The Library Instruction Cookbook

by Ryan L. Sittler and Douglas Cook

Association of College and Research Libraries
A division of the American Library Association
Chicago 2009

The paper used in this publication meets the minimum requirements of American National Standard for Information Sciences-Permanence of Paper for Printed Library Materials, ANSI Z39.48-1992. ∞

Library of Congress Cataloging-in-Publication Data

The library instruction cookbook / by Ryan L. Sittler and Douglas Cook.
    p. cm.
 ISBN 978-0-8389-8511-3 (pbk. : alk. paper) 1. Library orientation for college students--Case studies. I. Sittler, Ryan. II. Cook, Douglas, 1951-
 Z711.25.C65L53 2009
 025.5'677--dc22
                            2009022599

Printed in the United States of America.

13 12 11 10 09   5 4 3 2 1

TABLE OF CONTENTS

Preface

Every great meal needs a great dessert. OK, maybe *not* in a technical sense—but in the opinion of Your Humble Editors—it's a good idea. When we finished working on *Practical Pedagogy for Library Instructors: 17 Innovative Strategies to Improve Student Learning* we were still, in a word, hungry. We accomplished what we set out to do… but it felt like something was missing. (And, perhaps, Ryan was really hungry for chocolate-peanut butter ice cream.) (Gag, Doug likes Cherries Garcia.)

The Library Instruction Cookbook is, essentially, the dessert to our previous foray into the world of writing pragmatically about library instruction. To this end, we originally set out to come up with fifty practical approaches to library instruction (we overshot that mark by quite a bit!) We also wanted to find a way to make this information digestible so that it could be easily implemented by our loyal readers. Finally, we wanted to create something that did not require readers to be familiar with our previous book.

There are questions that we often ask ourselves (especially Doug, who has been an academic librarian for thirty-four years) and we think you probably have asked these questions, as well: How many times have you tried to get through to your students in your library instruction sessions and wished fervently that you could find some fresh new ideas to try? How many times have you been sitting in your cubby and received a phone call from a faculty member who wanted you to teach a class for his students tomorrow, and "No, they don't have an assignment?"

How many times have gotten tired of listening to yourself drone on to students about keywords, databases, limiters, Boolean operators ("Yawn"), inter-library loan, Google?, style manuals, the library Web page, Ask Me!, etc, etc. etc. and wished that you could find pedagogically sound activities which would help your students to learn without listening to you endlessly?

"Put that emotion in the food, because it's so much more rewarding down the line."
Gordon Ramsey, Chef and host of *Hell's Kitchen*

Hopefully, this book will help you fire up your grill, and then let the students do the cooking. Pedagogically, Ryan and Doug are Social Constructivists. We believe that students create their own knowledge during the interaction that occurs in a classroom. When you talk for fifty minutes, you give out information, but you do not give students the opportunity to create their own reality by engaging with new ideas, by talking to each other, and by talking to you. We believe that students learn through engagement. Contrary to the old maxim, "Too many chefs spoil the broth," we believe the opposite. In fact, without everybody in the kitchen acting as a Chef… you would not even have any broth.

"Get in zee keetchee und shoot yuoor muoot. Get zeem stoodents tu du zee vurk. Bork. Bork." The Swedish Chef

---

We have vetted every one of these recipes—making sure that contributing authors used only natural learning ingredients. (Sick of the puns yet? Don't worry, there will be more!)

Since we think students learn best by being actively involved, rather than by sitting and listening to Librarian-Speak for an hour, we selected recipes that limit librarian talk-time to about ten minutes or so. The cookbook includes a number of lesson planning and activity recipes that will help you to get started on your way to gourmet teaching.

It's hard to cook a great meal the first time you try a new recipe. And, we all wing instruction sessions from time to time (yes, us too!) (Doug flies far away sometimes.) But truly great instruction benefits from great preparation, great ingredients, and great execution. We hope this book can help you with the first two parts of that equation—and with practice, the execution should come quite naturally, too!

ACRL has never published anything like this before—and we could go on and on about the intricacies of putting it together… but like any good Chef's, we'd prefer to let our meal speak for itself. Without (very much) further ado…

Feel free to e-mail us if you have a comment or an idea for our next book.

Smile, learn, and above all else, enjoy! (Bon appétit!)

Your Humble ~~Editors~~ Chefs…
Ryan L. Sittler, California, PA, 2009
sittler@cup.edu

Doug Cook, Shippensburg, PA, 2009
dlcook@ship.edu

Acknowledgements

Chefs Ryan and Doug would like to thank our colleagues and Sous Chefs, worldwide, for their patience and assistance during the creation of this cookbook. We REALLY tested everybody's patience while working on this book—and thankfully, those kind folks stood by us when the going got tough!

Special thanks to Doug's daughter, Jen Cook, for helping us to get our ducks in a row. She did the first edit of all of these recipes and made sure they all had the correct subheadings. (The book would have been delayed at least two more months without her assistance.)

We also need to say thanks to Anne Marie Gruber, who early on sent us a recipe with the most fabulous foodie subheadings. Being the opportunistic (lazy?) editors we are, we asked her for permission to use her spicy subheadings (which you will see in every recipe) instead of our original, far more boring, subheadings. Thanks Anne Marie!

As always, thank you to Kathryn Deiss and Dawn Mueller at ACRL. Thanks to Dawn for encouraging Doug to learn Adobe Page-Maker (now InDesign) lo those many years ago, when he served as the Newsletter Editor for ACRL/EBSS. He put those skills to good use with this book.

Ryan would thank everyone if he could but… many thanks to Co-Chef Doug for picking up my slack when I dropped the ball, errr, spatula. Thanks to Gordon Ramsey for inspiring me to be critical while editing! And I'm also going to thank my sister, Shanon Sittler-Martin and former co-worker Patricia Nouhra—both of whom don't think I am going to mention them here. ☺ Finally, thanks to Heatherlee Smith for putting up with me when I was cranky from editing (and too tired to cook dinner… sorry, honey.)

Doug would like to thank Ryan for the idea for this crazy book. We were overwhelmed when we put out the call for our previous book—*Practical Pedagogy for Library Instructors*—and received hundreds of proposals, when we only needed fifteen or so. Ryan got extremely excited and said, "Let's do a book with a lot of short ideas for library instructors." Ryan also covered for me in the middle stages of the book's planning when I got snowed under with job-related projects. We seem to make a good team. I need to thank my wife, Carolyn, also a university faculty member, who understands this nutty urge we all have to write and edit. She also has the writing bug.

Thanks, of course, to the Swedish Chef from the Muppets who will ever remain an inspiration to us all when we cook, "Bork. Bork."

Finally, we would like to thank each of our recipe authors. What a talented bunch of librarians! These folks are the true Chefs in this cookbook. If someone really inspired you… we encourage you to e-mail them to let them know!

INTRODUCTION

Avoiding a Recipe for Disaster: Skirting Bad Instruction

Ryan L. Sittler, MSLS, MSIT

Allergy Warning

I will warn you ahead of time—this chapter contains no literature review. No bibliography. This is the only chapter in this book that is NOT in Chicago style. And I have not conducted formal research on the topic. If you have an allergy to this kind of information… stop now and jump to the first recipe. This chapter is, however, born from my education in instructional design, my opinions about teaching and learning, and my experience teaching in a library environment for roughly seven years. If you want quantitative research, you will be disappointed—however—if you want some qualitative insight into instruction… please read on.

Introduction

If I told you, today, that you had to cook a large, complex meal from scratch—without a recipe or formal training—you would probably be a little nervous. You might know, for example, that you need rice to make risotto… but did you know that *true* risotto needs to be prepared in a specific way? Otherwise, it is *just* a food made with rice.

You could go through all of the stress of studying the recipe, gathering the ingredients, cooking the food, and serving it to your guests… and even though your diners may eat your food… without previous practice or training you might still have a disaster on your hands. The same concept holds true for instruction. If you have never taken coursework or training in *how* to teach… you may have a difficult time coming up with a delicious recipe that will tantalize your learners' taste buds.

Whether it is a bad recipe or bad instruction… you are not going to stay in business very long if you cannot put out a quality product. "But," you might be asking, "everyone has a different teaching style and emphasizes different things while teaching… what works for one person doesn't necessarily work for another… so how do you know if you're approach is good or bad? And if it's bad… how do you fix it?" Put on your *toque blanche*, grab your apron, and I'll be happy to answer your questions…

So What *IS* Bad Instruction?

The concepts of *good instruction* versus *bad instruction* are not always easily defined—because instructional approaches that do not work under one circumstance might work under another. Therefore, we will discuss these ideas in generalities. Let's look at bad food first. Bad food can taste terrible, be presented poorly, and even make your diners ill. Good food, on the other hand, looks appetizing, tastes exquisite, and makes you want to come back for more. The same rules, essentially, apply to instruction.

Bad instruction, like bad food, is poorly accepted by the audience. I would define *bad instruction* as any instructional situation in which your learners are not learning (most of) the information/concepts you want them to learn. Your instructional goals and objectives are not met. You may even turn your learners *off* to the information/concepts being presented during the course of the instructional situation. Bad instruction can have the same impact as bad food—it may put you right out of business.

Good instruction, like good food, hits the spot. You could say that *good instruction* has taken place when your learners are learning (most of) the information/concepts you want them to learn. Your instructional goals and objectives are met. And, just maybe, you even turn your learners *on* to the information/concepts being presented during the course of the instructional situation—and they are jazzed at the idea of learning more. Good instruction keeps your learners coming back for more.

The reality of the situation is that your instruction will probably live somewhere in the middle of these extremes. Like a good chef who has an occasional disaster, you cannot expect every learner, in all situations, to learn *everything*. But you can design your instruction in such a way that the majority of your learners acquire most of the information/concepts you intended for them to learn.

What's So Bad About Bad Instruction?

Most of us do not have the advantage of having been taught how to teach. Or at the least, we may not have been taught how to teach *well*. Yet, we place an expectation on ourselves that simply because we know how to do something—searching databases, for example—that we should be able to teach it well. This is not necessarily true. No chef (except maybe Gordon Ramsey) ever made a great meal the first time they turned on the stove. It takes training and lots of practice to be great…

But does it matter if we can teach things well? My argument, of course, is yes. It does matter. But why? If learners are exposed to the information—whether the delivery method is imperfect or not is irrelevant… right? Right? Food is nourishing whether it tastes good or not? Right?

What, exactly, is so *bad* about bad instruction? There are really two factors at play. For starters:

People do not learn as much from bad instruction.

A learner has to *try* not to learn a thing from you, even on your worst day, regardless of what you are teaching. But, they may not learn much at all. If they are not learning from you, they are probably also disengaged. And in this case:

A learner disengaged is a learner lost.

It is difficult to energize someone about a subject that they find cumbersome. (Are you, dear reader, interested in learning some trigonometry right now?) When you disengage your learner from the learning process… you may be inadvertently turn-ing them off to the subject matter at hand. They will confuse their lack of interest in the instructional strategy—for lack of interest in the subject. Moreover, this can be a negative, and long-lasting, association. Why do so many good restaurants with great potential go out of business? Because first impressions can destroy a business. Diners, like learners, go to where they perceive the situation to be better… and it might not be your classroom.

Good instruction, fortunately, will have the opposite impact of those two statements outlined above. People learn quite a bit from good instruction… and if they are engaged, they will come back for more.

Being Realistic: The 10 And 10 Rule

You should always strive for 100 percent learning to take place for 100 percent of your learners. Nevertheless, be prepared to accept that this is usually not possible and you will—like it or not—reach a smaller number of people. (This is particularly true if you are trying to present a large amount of information in short period.) Not everyone has the same taste in food—pizza may be your favorite food and the person sitting beside you may prefer filet mignon. The same truth applies to instructional strategies—not everyone likes the same thing.

Imagine cooking a meal for thirty people. Unfortunately, you agreed to cook the meal without finding out what anybody likes. Even at your best, you will have to guess at what people are going to enjoy. You cook an elaborate French meal, using every super-secret technique that you know, and you think to yourself "Wow, I've created a fantastic meal here!" True, until an American Little League Team comes walking in… fresh from practice… wanting hot dogs and hamburgers. This is an extreme example, but it does illustrate a good point—you cannot just predict what people are hungry for. Likewise, you cannot just predict how people prefer to learn. You will (usually) be designing your instruction in a bit of a "haze." And so you cannot expect to reach 100 percent of your audience… even on your best day.

I use something I call the "10 and 10 Rule" to keep me aware of my learners and, by extension, my teaching environment. (Ok, it is not a true rule… more of a reality check.) The rule is: given 100 learners, assume 10 will eat up every word you say and 10 will ignore you even if you are (literally) on fire and juggling chainsaws… everyone else will be somewhere in the middle.

I call the first 10 learners the *True Believers*. They enjoy learning for learning's sake. Their faces are smiley and they are prepared to learn. These learners are interested in consuming any knowledge you wish to share… and will make a concerted effort, regardless of your pedagogical technique, to learn and adapt. These folks are your aficionados, the diners who are regulars at your restaurant. They will eat anything you feed them and love every bite.

I call the last 10 learners the *Skeptics*. They are not interested in what you have to say. Period. Their arms are folded… and their expression is that of "prove it to me." They could be excellent students and very interested, under normal circumstances… but they are having a bad day and do not feel like listening to you. Regardless of what pedagogical technique you employ… they will fight you every step of the way. No matter what you do, these folks will complain about their meal—and go to the restaurant across the street. They just do not *want* to like your cooking. They are your worst critics.

I call the middle 80 learners the *Tolerators.* These folks are going to wait-watch-and-see. They will exhibit characteristics of those at both ends of the spectrum. They will start out in the middle and may gravitate to one of the extremes before the session has ended. In other words, these folks will come to your restaurant and will give your grub an honest chance. They could become your regulars, as well.

Again, the "10 and 10 Rule" is a general observation and not a fixed rule. But by using it as a reality check during instruction sessions… it makes it easier for me to assess what is happening in the classroom.

Seek Answers In The Questions…

If you are reading this book, you are interested in being a better teacher. Moreover, you are probably a great teacher already. However, I know there are some folks out there that need me to convince them of what I am saying… and I can understand why. But whether you agree with me or disagree with me… I have an exercise for you to try.

Even if you are the best teacher you know—ask yourself the following questions. Be honest… write down your answers… and

reflect on what you come up with:

- Were you taught *how* to teach well—or did you just kind of *pick up* approaches, strategies, and concepts along the way?
- Do you really *know* whether you are doing a good job of teaching? *How*?
- Are you being evaluated by people that are knowledgeable enough to *know* whether or not you are doing a good job of teaching?
- Is your teaching based on real *pedagogically sound choices*—or *your personal opinion* about what you *assume* makes for good teaching?
- Are you teaching in the *best way* to reach your learners—or are you teaching in the way that *makes you most comfortable*?

Teaching is like cooking: it is about choices that inform your technique. Are your choices regarding content, preparation, and audience needs influenced by what is best for your target audience—or what is best for you? This dichotomy can mean the difference between instruction that earns applause… and instruction that leaves your learners confused and uncomfortable in the classroom.

If you make yourself responsible for your own teaching—if you re-evaluate what you are doing and how you are trying to do it—you can always feel comfortable in knowing that you are doing your best at that moment.

How do you feel about your responses to the questions I posed? Even if you were completely content with your answers, I

would recommend asking yourself these questions throughout your career. It will help to keep you fresh—and if you are fresh—you are relevant.

So, How About Some Tips for Designing Instruction?

Entire books have been written about instructional design since the 1970's (few as thoroughly done as *The Systematic Design of Instruction* by Walter Dick, Lou Carey, and James O. Carey. This book is a cumbersome read… and was not easy for me to get through… but I cannot deny the long-lasting and positive impact it has had on me.) I would never attempt to recapture the full body of knowledge in instructional design in just a few bullet points… but I still want to give you something that you can use. So instead, the following points are tips on how you can improve your instruction in the short-term. If you are interested in improving your instruction in the long-term… you will need to read a few books on instructional design or, better yet, take a class on the subject.

Sittler's Simple Suggestions for Improving Instruction:

- Know "why" you are doing something—are you teaching things that are relevant to the learning situation, or simply because you "always" teach these things?
- Keep it simple—eliminate jargon unless it is necessary for learning. Eliminate complex concepts unless absolutely needed for learning.
- Separate the "nice to know" from the "need to know"—unless you have 16

weeks to teach a topic, you cannot teach everything. Eliminate items that are not "core" to what you are teaching.

- Be mindful of time, human attention span, and learning theory—keep presentations short, with plenty of time for practical application.
- Remember that it is better to teach one thing well than five things poorly—identify three main concepts that are "core" to your learning situation and teach them well.
- Adjust your teaching to your time and not your time to the teaching—in other words, if you have 50 minutes to teach… teach 50 minutes worth of material. Do not force three hours worth of material simply because you want to get it all in.
- Teach learners what they need to know to get through their immediate assignment (unless you have a more robust information literacy program in place.) Learners will tend to ignore things that seem irrelevant to the assignment.

Will This Book Help Me to Create "Good" Instruction?

The simple answer is… maybe. The recipes in this book can provide you with a start. As with any recipe from any cookbook, you—the chef—make all the difference. Practice and actively listen to your audience. They are your clientele… and they will be very vocal if you allow them to be.

The better your instruction is designed, the better your instruction will be delivered, and the better the experience for your learners. You might even earn some applause. And remember: when you are trimming things down or trying to be innovative… it is not pandering to students…

It is just good instructional design. Bon appétit!

1. LIBRARY ORIENTATION

Whipping up an Appetite for Academic Journals

Students about to enter university in the Fall are given a crash course to prepare them for college life. This recipe will help students to learn to find journals in the library.

Jacqui Weetman DaCosta, Information Literacy Librarian, The College of New Jersey, NJ, dacosta@tcnj.edu

NUTRITION INFORMATION

This recipe was created to whip up interest in the library for a group of Educational Opportunity Fund (EOF) students who attend the college on a six-week summer program, prior to entering as Freshmen in the Fall. As this group is verbal and active, the recipe mixes discussion and guided activities. This recipe gives students some practical experience of finding scholarly journal articles using electronic and print resources. Typically, these are students who may have little or no concept about what a journal looks, smells, or feels like. The principal aim is for them to get their hands dirty identifying the raw ingredients needed for success.

COOKING TIME

Cooking time for this recipe is 2 hours and serves twenty students.

ACRL INFORMATION DIETARY STANDARDS ADDRESSED

Standard One: 1.1, 1.2.
Standard Two: 2.2, 2.3, 2.4, 2.5.
Standard Four: 4.2, 4.3.

MAIN COOKING TECHNIQUE

Mini-demonstration, students working in pairs doing hands-on exercises, active participation, moving around the library

MAIN INGREDIENTS

- Computer access for all students
- Instructor's station
- Blackboard / Whiteboard
- Easy access to print journals

PREPARATION

Students are required to complete modules from the library's online tutorial each week. The instruction session is timed to coincide with their completion of the module on Finding Articles in Research Databases. You will need to prepare searches and handouts on relevant topics.

THE INSTRUCTION SESSION

1. Introduction
   a. Ask students how they currently do research.
   b. Using a relevant topic, ask the students to suggest some keywords.
   c. Explain the importance of using databases and ask students to select relevant subject categories from a list on the library web pages.
   d. Demonstrate a relevant subject search showing how to limit to scholarly journal articles.

2. Hands-on Search
   a. Electronic Journal—Distribute handouts to guide students through a search on their own topic for which they need to provide a citation to a relevant article found electronically.

b. Print Journal—Upon presentation of an electronic citation to the instructor, students are assigned to work in pairs to find an article in a print journal. They are given clues on a handout but need to find the call number, by using the library catalog, then locate and retrieve the actual journal from the shelves.

ALLERGY WARNINGS

- This group can be like a James Bond Martini—Shaken Not Stirred—as they are excitable but are not likely to be turned on by library research! The challenge is to whet their appetite and turn the research into a game where there are prizes (mini candy bars) for those who retrieve the correct electronic and print journal articles.
- The activities are deliberately active so this is not the kind of instruction session for the fainthearted or someone who likes a quiet classroom!
- The students often have trouble interpreting call numbers, and finding the print journals on the shelves, which is why pairing them up is important.

CHEF'S NOTE

Students are required to complete regular blog entries for this course, which is a good way for the instructor to assess their reactions to, and reflections on, the library session. One student commented: "Today's library session was very helpful… I still wish you were there to see the enthusiasm that your students had. I learned some new ways to research topics and even found some ideas on my topic. I never used those ways and databases so I really took good notes and used my time wisely."

A pre- and post-course assessment was also undertaken, in which students were asked, "Where do you feel that you have learned most of the skills which helped you to answer the questions above?" Before starting the online tutorial and attending the library session—56.3 percent felt that they had "just learned them on my own." At the end of the course—only 14.8 percent felt that they had "just learned them on my own." A whopping 80.4 percent felt that they had learned the skills from a combination of the online tutorial and the library instruction session!

READ Posters: A Favorite Mezze with a Middle Eastern Flavor

This recipe, which can be part of freshmen orientation, gets the students into the library, exploring the stacks, and meeting the staff. Incorporating Arabic language into the poster is a way of acknowledging and respecting the local culture.

Nancy Fawley, Reference Librarian, Virginia Commonwealth University in Qatar, nfawley@qatar.vcu.edu

NUTRITION INFORMATION

Virginia Commonwealth University in Qatar is a branch campus of the American university's School of the Arts located in the Middle East. Instruction is in English and most of the students speak English as a second language. Many have had little to no experience using a library. This activity can be done at any time for any student group, but in this case it was used as part of the freshman orientation activities before the start of the fall semester.

COOKING TIME

Small groups of ten or less visited the library for about 45 minutes at a time. The school is small and the freshman class averages about fifty students. An afternoon was scheduled for the activity.

ACRL INFORMATION DIETARY STANDARDS ADDRESSED

Standard One: 1.1, 1.2, 1.3.
Standard Two: 2.1.

MAIN COOKING TECHNIQUE

Hands-on activity

MAIN INGREDIENTS

- Backdrop with the word Read written in English and Arabic.
- Photographer
- Upbeat and approachable staff
- Books, to be chosen by the student
- Laser photo paper to print the posters (optional)
- For garnish: A giveaway, such as a pen with the library's Web address, or a prize drawing. (We had a drawing for a gift certificate to Starbucks.)

PREPARATION

If this *mezze* (appetizer) activity is part of freshman orientation, it is important to have the activity put on the official schedule in order to be promoted. The backdrop must be designed and printed. We used the university's graphic designer to make ours but ALA also sells software to make READ posters. The photographer must be booked well in advance

and, if you are distributing handouts or giveaways, those must be created or purchased ahead of time, too. The day of the event, the area where the photos are to be taken must be set up. Purchase high quality paper to print the posters on if you choose to distribute the photos that way. Also, this is an opportunity to promote the library and its services, so be prepared to talk about this with the students.

Photo of Yafea Al-faqieh, Virginia Commonwealth University in Qatar, class of 2012. Photographer Markus Elblaus, VCU Qatar

INSTRUCTION SESSION

1. Greet the students and explain the event.

2. Have the students choose a book to be photographed with. Students may need assistance finding the book in the online catalog and on the shelf. Others may want some suggestions or help finding a book on a particular topic. This is the students' first experience with their university's library. Remember, first impressions count.

3. The photographer takes the picture.

4. The photo can be printed or e-mailed to the student. Some editing on Photoshop may be required.

ALLERGY WARNINGS

Many Muslims, especially women in this conservative country, do not want their photos taken and it is extremely important to respect their decision. Regardless of whether or not students want to have their photo taken, the activity is still an opportunity to introduce the library and its services.

CHEF'S NOTE

When I introduced the READ poster activity to the first group of freshman I got ten sets of blank stares and I thought, "What was I thinking to propose this event?" Later I found out this was more a case of first-day-of-school jitters than a reaction to my activity. Many did not want their photo taken, but there were enough who did to make it enjoyable. And those who did not pose for the camera were active bystanders, helping their new classmates and friends choose a book.

It was very social; the students were bonding with each other and with us. We talked about reading, books, and studying design. I knew it was a success when students came back to the library at the end of the day to say goodbye. The benefit of the activity became more apparent as the semester progressed. All the freshmen knew me by name and have an understanding of the role that the library and I play in the university. It set the foundation for all my subsequent interactions with them.

The notoriety of the READ poster has grown and I am looking forward to repeating the activity for a new group of students. The banner currently stands outside of the library boldly suggesting to our visitors to READ, in the language of their choice.

An Eight-Course Library Meal

A banquet for First-Year-Students! This recipe has small groups of students learn and then teach each other about the library.

Alison Gregory, Instructional Services Librarian and Assistant Professor, Snowden Library, Lycoming College, Williamsport, PA, gregory@lycoming.edu

NUTRITION INFORMATION

This eight-course meal is intended for first-year students who are getting their first taste of the library: a smorgasbord of resources, if you will! The purpose is to provide students with an overview of the types of resources available in and through the library. Eight groups of students become the experts on particular library resources. Each group then shares that information with the larger class.

COOKING TIME

Cooking time is 50 minutes. Recipe serves sixteen to twenty-four students. The subject or discipline addressed can vary, but the flavors really complement English composition classes or First-Year Seminars.

ACRL INFORMATION DIETARY STANDARDS ADDRESSED

Standard One: 1.2.
Standard Two: 2.1, 2.2, 2.3.
Standard Four: 4.3.

MAIN COOKING TECHNIQUE

Small-group work, peer instruction, structured jigsaw

MAIN INGREDIENTS

- Computer lab
- Instructor's station
- Worksheets for each group
- Note-taking booklet/handout for each student

PREPARATION

This session requires a fair amount of advanced preparation, as it relies on eight very structured worksheets for the student presenters. To kick up the flavor of the session, each student should also receive a booklet about the resources, but instead of giving them the information, include lots of fill-in-the-blanks and empty bullet points for them to complete as their peers present the information.

THE INSTRUCTION SESSION

1. Welcome students to the library—1 minute.
2. Tell students that the goal for the class is to have them become familiar with the relevant, appropriate resources for the upcoming assignments in this class. They will all be familiar with how to use the online catalog and how to physically locate a book; how to use a few of the most commonly used databases; how and when to use the reference collection materials; how to evaluate Web sites; how to locate periodicals; and how to request materials from other libraries—4 minutes.
3. Break class into eight groups. Each group will be working on one worksheet.
4. Give the groups 5 minutes to do the tasks listed on their worksheets.
5. Have each group designate a spokesperson who will teach the group's resource(s) to the rest of the class in a 4 minute segment.
6. Give every student a copy of the note-taking booklet and instruct them to fill in the blanks as their peers present the information.

7. Student presentations can be accomplished by either having the spokespeople come to the front of the room to use the instructor's computer and projector, or have the students remain at their computers and utilize a classroom control software system such as SMARTSync.

8. Guide the student presenters through their portions as needed. Make any necessary additions (or corrections) to the information after each student presenter has finished.

ALLERGY WARNINGS

- Students whose worksheet exercises require them to physically retrieve an item may balk at having to get up and "walk all the way up the stairs."

AN EIGHT-COURSE LIBRARY MEAL THE MENU

Group 1—Reference Collection
Group 2—Online Catalog and E-ZBorrow
Group 3—Periodicals
Group 4—Academic Search Elite Database
Group 5—Newspaper Source Database and WorldCat
Group 6—LexisNexis and New York Times Historical Backfile Databases
Group 7—Library Web Site
Group 8—Web Site Evaluation and Boolean Operators

CHEF'S NOTE

Most students seem to enjoy the activity because it is totally student hands-on and librarian mouth-shut. They become fairly adept with at least one resource and are exposed, by their peers, to many other resources. I encourage them to ask each other questions both during the library session and afterward.

Faculty members really like the approach, since it gives the students immediate experience and it provides an opportunity for informal public speaking.

There is a lot of preparation involved, but the eight worksheets can be easily adapted to subject-specific courses. In addition to the freshman composition courses, I've had great success using this with a 200-level religion class.

The note-taking booklet and eight worksheets are available online. http://srv2.lycoming.edu/~gregory/Library_Instruction_Handouts/

Basic Appetizers with a Twist

This recipe is one of many approaches to a one-shot session that introduces the library's menu of resources and services and at the same time engages first-year and transfer students in preparation for future academic research and life-long learning skills.

Cindy Gruwell, St. Cloud State University, cagruwell@stcloudstateuniversity.edu

NUTRITION INFORMATION
Too often, our one-shot library instruction (LI) sessions miss the mark by either overwhelming students with too much information and/or not engaging them with interactive activities. The best LI sessions provide a strong first impression by informing students about the basic resources and services your individual library has to offer.

COOKING TIME
This session will engage and entice thirty freshmen and transfer students with a 50 minute light and tasty overview of library services and resources in an interactive hands-on kitchen environment.

ACRL INFORMATION DIETARY STANDARDS ADDRESSED
Standard One.
Standard Two.

MAIN COOKING TECHNIQUE
Short demonstration (using a short version of the "Cephalonian Method"), ten spicy questions, and a hands-on session

MAIN INGREDIENTS
- One excited and energetic librarian chef extraordinaire
- One classroom kitchen nook with computers for up to thirty students
- One or more professors/teaching assistant sous-chefs
- One Web-based library menu for appetizer selection and demonstration
- A wide variety of information resources for personalized dipping!
- Optional: 10 spicy questions to promote an interactive discourse

PREPARATION
Ask students to review the library orientation video posted online.
Touch base with the professor to discuss menu items.
Collect and review three well-nourished handouts including: Library 101 Overview, a building map, and a hands-on recipe contest (exercise sheet) challenging the students to find appetizer ingredients.
Prepare Web Course Guide where appropriate, e.g. **http://research.stcloudstate.edu/page.phtml?page_id=34**

INSTRUCTION SESSION
1. Welcome and overview of the days' session—5 mins.
2. Distribute spicy questions on color-coded index cards with prepared questions that correlate with the appetizer topics.
3. Present PowerPoint of crudités (major resource points)—15 mins.
4. Invite questions, if and when you are met with silence, call on a holder of a spicy question—10 mins.
5. Time to get the hands dirty—begin the ingredient contest—20 mins.
6. Note: A librarian chef extraordinaire should roam and assist trainees
7. In closing, remind the students that there is more to cooking than meets the eye. They are welcome to consult with the chef and/or members of the cooking school (Reference) at any time!

ALLERGY WARNINGS

Some students may exhibit boredom (They already know this stuff!) or itchy computer fingers that find inappropriate recipe ingredients. To combat this you may either invite them to turn off the monitor during demonstrations, or better yet send the presentation to their desktop for that up close and personal feel.

CHEF'S NOTE

Making library orientations interesting and satisfying can sometimes defy the odds, but with the right ingredients this can be an informative and positive experience. Using a blend of demonstration mixed with meaningful hands-on activities allows student to practice their culinary skills and receive immediate feedback from their roving chef extraordinaire. The presence of the class professor during the session is very important.

Although challenging, one-shot library instruction sessions can be quite satisfying. Whether spontaneous, or prompted by a spicy question, it is the responsibility of librarian chefs to create interesting sessions and serve up an ample amount of appetizers to whet our students' appetites. Using the "Cephalonian Method" is just one way to actively engage both the naturally inquisitive student and their aloof counterparts. I have found this process makes a significant difference in both delivery and maintaining student interest. A challenge we as professionals face every day.

So, You've Visited the Library for Instruction Before? Prove it!

We have all encountered it—the phrase "I've learned this already" as students file into the classroom. This recipe provides an opportunity for students to refine their research skills while recognizing the fact that many have visited the library for basic instruction before.

Lauren Jensen, Public Services Librarian, Hewes Library, Monmouth College, Monmouth, Illinois, ljensen@monm.edu

NUTRITION INFORMATION

This recipe refreshes students' memories concerning library resources and faculty members are satisfied that their classes have demonstrated a working knowledge of the library by the time students leave. We recommend that this exercise be reserved for upper class students with more advanced information literacy skills. Most liberal arts subjects can be modified to fit the exercise.

COOKING TIME

Cooking time is 60 minutes. Serves any number of students.

ACRL INFORMATION DIETARY STANDARDS ADDRESSED

Standard One: 1.1, 1.2, 1.4.
Standard Two: 2.1, 2.2, 2.3, 2.4.

MAIN COOKING TECHNIQUE

Small group work, short demonstrations, peer-to-peer contributions, and brief presentations

MAIN INGREDIENTS

- Instructor's station
- Computers for students
- Review questions
- Bowl or bag from which students can draw questions

PREPARATION

Consult with the instructor about key resources or themes that need to be reviewed. Compile a list of review questions before the students arrive. Print questions out so students can draw a review question. Print an additional copy of all questions to have at the instructor's console.

THE INSTRUCTION SESSION

1. Reiterate the fact that you know students have been to the library before and that they are here today to demonstrate how much they remember. Explain the outline for the research session. Students will work independently and then with a partner to determine the answers to their review questions. In the second half of the class period, the pairs will share their experiences with the class.

2. Have students draw a review question and sit in pairs. Allow approximately 5 mins. for each student to individually research the answer to their review question and write down the steps taken to locate the answer. Circulate among the students to answer any questions. Questions can vary from "Does the library own this journal?" to "How do I know if the library owns a copy of *A Tale of Two Cities*?" to "I'm looking for a 19th century book review. Where do I find that?" Question difficulty should correspond to the skill level of the class and the resources the professor wants to cover.

3. Have students swap questions and begin answering their partner's review question—5 mins.

4. Students compare answers to the review questions, noting differences or similarities—5 mins.

5. From your list, begin a review of the questions with the full class. Ask students to present their review question, demonstrate the method of retrieving the answer, and results of their discussion with their partner. Interject pointers or quick demonstrations if needed.

6. Reserve a few minutes at the end of the class period for questions or clarifications.

ALLERGY WARNINGS

Some students may complain about the questions they draw. If additional questions are available after everyone has drawn, they may redraw.

CHEF'S NOTE

In the session's first half, many students are surprised that their partners do not begin their research the same way. In the second half of the session, students have the opportunity to suggest alternative methods of retrieving the information and to comment on their peers' work. This session can be personalized to any subject and is especially helpful if the professor wants students to review a certain resource before beginning a project. The librarian and faculty member can work together to ensure that some questions revolve around that resource.

If there is time remaining at the end of the period, especially long class periods, I let students play "Stump the Librarian" where they devise the questions. Time can also be used to go over a particularly difficult process or resource that students had difficulty with in the beginning of the session.

Book 'Em!

This recipe is an information mystery scavenger hunt based on the Clue board game.

Lilia Murray, Murray State University, lilia.murray@murraystate.edu

NUTRITION INFORMATION
This light recipe exposes students to a possibly unfamiliar palette, the Library of Congress Classification System, while introducing them to the library locale.

COOKING TIME
The recipe calls for twenty freshman or new students for a one hour session.

ACRL INFORMATION DIETARY STANDARDS ADDRESSED
Standard One: 1.1, 1.2, 1.3.
Standard Two: 2.1, 2.2, 2.3, 2.4.
Standard Four: 4.1.
Standard Five: 5.2.

MAIN COOKING TECHNIQUE
Interactive discovery and small group work

MAIN INGREDIENTS
- Masking tape, pencils, sticky notes, colored stickers
- Computer and internet access
- Library cards (at least one per group), library maps
- Four Initial clue e-mails, additional clues, red herrings
- Various resource formats (books, computers, microfilm, DVDs, etc.)

Optional ingredients if you intend to become a detective
- Detective's costume
- Fake badge
- Name tag
- Notepad with pencil
- "Do Not Enter" Security Tape
- Other members of the "force" (librarians)

PREPARATION
- Compose the victim's last four e-mails
- Create four different clue routes, color coded by circle stickers
- Prepare and place clues and red herrings
- Outline body on floor with masking tape
- Optional: Secure the area with the "Do Not Enter" security tape and get into costume

THE INSTRUCTION SESSION
Rather than a librarian lecturer, students arrive finding an appetizer: **the outline of a body on the floor**. A brief scream is given to get their attention and to let them know that this information meal is about to be served. The librarian detective (optional: a la Inspector Clouseau) then makes his/her appearance and provides a brief background to the case:

"Late last night, library staff were surprised to find the twisted body of Stu Denwurka in the library. The sophomore seemed to have been getting a head start on his research paper; however, his laptop and book bag were missing. Four friends have come forward with cryptic e-mails from Stu, sent shortly before his body was discovered.

You have been called to the scene to help solve the mystery. We have reason to suspect the act occurred elsewhere in this building and the body was eventually moved here into the lobby. Thus, the answer to this "whodunit" requires three parts:
1. Suspect — Who Did It?
2. Device — With What Object?
3. Room — In Which Room?
If you run into any difficulties, you may ask me for help. I'll be at the reference desk—that's where you go for help when you're in the library."

- The students are then divided into four color-coded teams, each group receiving an e-mail leading to different sets of library clues and red herrings. Each trail takes students through major areas of the library to locate various resources and answers the questions listed above. The last clue ends in the OPAC with an additional final description in an entry.

Characters include:
- Anita Buk
- Bib ReCord
- Dewey Dooit
- Ivana Czechitowt
- Kenya Renu
- O. C. Elsie
- OPAC Shakur
- Perry Adickelle
- Stu Denwurka
- w.ILL.iam

ALLERGY WARNINGS
- Clues and red herrings may inadvertently be reshelved or checked out by other patrons, so be sure to inform other librarians and staff of your recipe activity.
- It is important to have different sets of e-mails and color-coded clues; otherwise, groups will just follow each other around.
- Some students may sit this out, opting for social time. It's helpful to have a member of your force bounce between all groups and follow their progress.
- All areas and items should be handicap accessible.

CHEF'S NOTE
- This session can be as dramatic or as low-key as you want. You can even recruit colleagues to act out parts.
- Students seem to appreciate you going the extra mile for them and love that you're willing to make a fool of yourself. Typically, the goofier the detective, the better the response.
- Although students work in teams, some individuals may still be unenthusiastic about this activity. Incentives like chocolate bars or free copy cards to the winning team may alleviate any lack of interest.

Einstein's Universe

This recipe features library-related scenarios, loosely based on the life of Albert Einstein, which are tackled by teams of students.

Robert Schroeder, Reference and Instruction Librarian, Portland State University, schroedr@pdx.edu

NUTRITION INFORMATION

For most of these students this class is their first introduction to a college library and college-level research. The students work in teams on simple-to-solve library scenarios. After discovering the answer each team must then use SMART Board technology to present their solution to the class.

In this class I have not only cognitive goals for the students regarding effective research, but I also have many affective goals relating to their feelings and experience of the library and the confusing array of library databases

Their ultimate assignment is to write a brief research paper about anything related to the life and times of Albert Einstein.

COOKING TIME

Cooking time for this recipe is 60 to 90 minutes and serves about thirty students.

ACRL INFORMATION DIETARY STANDARDS ADDRESSED

Standard Two: 2.2, 2.3.

MAIN COOKING TECHNIQUE

Team work, jigsaw

MAIN INGREDIENTS

- A classroom with four to six tables (preferably circular).
- Computers (laptops) for each student. Four to six laptops on each table.
- A SMART Board at the head of the class with a Bluetooth enabled keyboard.

PREPARATION

Your primary preparation before the class is to understand what the most important student learning goals are. Since you can't cover everything they need to know you must narrow to the four to five most important skills they need in order to take the next steps in their research.

Your next step is creating individual activities that would allow the students to evidence these goals. Create as many activities as you have tables (teams), and make them take roughly the same amount of time to complete—10 minutes. Write them up as scenarios on a handout that each student will get in class.

THE INSTRUCTION SESSION

1. Introduce the sessions's goals.

2. The students at each table become a research team and are given a research scenario to complete.

3. Each team works to discover ways to complete its scenario. The students are told they will be coming up to the SMART Board to share what they have learned with the rest of the class.

4. Use the SMART Board to show the students where to start their research.

5. Circulate from table to table, as needed, to help with questions as they arise.

6. After each team has completed their scenario, they report how and what they found to the rest of the class. Chime in as needed to highlight points they might have missed.

7. For the time remaining in the class each student can search for information relevant to their own topic.

ALLERGY WARNINGS

- Because this is an activity rather than a lecture/demo the learning goals must be accordingly pared down in number.

- The locus of control to some extent is also given over to the students during the times they report back to their classmates on what they've found. This and the general rambunctiousness at using the SMART Board can be unnerving for the instructor the first few times.

- The instructor also has to be cognizant of when to allow students to follow dead ends or play around with the technology, and when to draw them back to the task at hand. Some chaos can work well to support the affective goals of the class.

CHEF'S NOTE

Most of the students I have in Einstein's Universe seem to enjoy working in groups. Also knowing that they and their group have a task to perform and will be teaching the results to the class in 10 minutes, grabs their attention from the very beginning of the class.

The technology of the SMART Board seems especially intriguing to them. Using the SMART Board excites them and pulls them into the lesson. They not only have fun presenting to their classmates, but I also constantly see signs that, by coming up to the SMART Board and teaching the class, they begin to recognize and value each other as teachers as well as classmates.

Social constructivist theory is also highlighted. The students themselves come up with their own solutions to the research scenarios presented. Their ideas often are different than the instructor's way of doing things, but students are shown as being able to create their own solutions to problems.

One of the great benefits of having active team-based exercises is that the students are doing the work and essentially teaching the class. The librarian acts as a facilitator. This teaching method also affords the librarian a lot of time to observe student learning in the classroom and see what is working and what isn't. It makes both formative and summative assessment much easier to do.

Scenario 6.626068

Your classmate recommended a book of love letters that Einstein wrote to a woman named Mileva Maric.

1. Does PSU own this book?
2. What is the call number?
3. Is it available for check out at this time?
4. What floor of the library is it located on?
5. Is this book available in the Summit catalog?

Scenario mc²

Being somewhat of a scientist yourself, you want to perform a quantum information experiment on the PSU Book Catalog (VIKAT). You will search on permutations of Einstein.

Do a subject search for Einstein.
1. How many related subjects did you find?
2. How many books did you find?

Do an author search on Einstein.
3. How many books did Albert Einstein write?

Do a keyword search on Einstein.
4. How many books did you find?

Discuss and share with the class.
5. Which is the best search?

Ethnographers for an Hour

This recipe asks students to become ethnographers, by observing and recording what goes on in the library.

Nancy Noe, Instruction Coordinator, Auburn University, noenanc@auburn.edu

NUTRITION INFORMATION

While traditional library tours are often requested (and given), library faculty have come to realize that those interactions are neither satisfying nor effective, either for themselves or the students. Working within a framework of student-centered and active learning, librarians created the "Ethnographer for an Hour" tour. Students wander, observe and speak with library inhabitants, take field notes, and then share their findings with each other. Individuals with camera phones are asked to take pictures and e-mail images to the librarian leading the expedition.

COOKING TIME

Cooking time is 60 minutes and serves one class.

ACRL INFORMATION DIETARY STANDARDS ADDRESSED

Standard Two: 2.3.

MAIN COOKING TECHNIQUE

Student-directed small groups

MAIN INGREDIENTS

Blank floor maps, clipboards, pens. Document camera (or ability to project floor maps and field notes)

PREPARATION

- Copies of floor maps
- Copies of handouts

THE INSTRUCTION SESSION

1. Students are divided into groups (corresponding with the number of floors in the library) and given blank floor maps to use for field notes.
2. Ethnography is explained and activity handout provided. Students are given 20 minutes to complete the assignment and reconvene in an instruction lab.
3. Each group presents their findings to the class as a whole, and the librarian highlights important resources/services with an emphasis on help points.

ALLERGY WARNINGS

Be prepared for shy groups. Be prepared to supplement any important aspect that students may have overlooked. Prepare the entire library for the event (more than one class has stumbled into cataloging!)

CHEF'S NOTE

Students love engaging in this activity and are happy not to be following a librarian around the library for a tour. If you don't have a large library, consider breaking your library into sections/areas. Or you can also scale the concept to library homepage exploration.

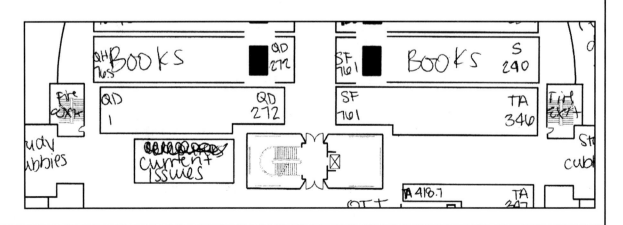

The Librarian, the Web, and the Wardrobe: The Library Homepage as a Portal to *Librarnia*

Using the Web page as a portal to a new world, small groups of new students learn about the library and teach their new-found knowledge to the rest of the class.

Emaly Conerly, Carson-Newman College, econerly@cn.edu and Kelli Williams, Carson-Newman College, kwilliams@cn.edu

NUTRITION INFORMATION

Introduce students to the fascinating world of *Librarnia* (or, as some call it, the Library). This session allows freshmen to get acquainted with the Library by exploring the Library's homepage on the Web. Students collaborate with each other in groups, and then teach their peers a portion of the homepage.

COOKING TIME

Cooking time is 60 minutes and serves twenty-five new students.

ACRL INFORMATION DIETARY STANDARDS ADDRESSED

Standard Two: 2.1, 2.3, 2.4.

MAIN COOKING TECHNIQUE

Jigsaw technique, group work

MAIN INGREDIENTS

- Computer lab
- Handouts
- Old-fashioned yardstick or pointing device
- Gummy worms (Book Worms) for rewards to groups as they finish teaching their peers

PREPARATION

- Print handouts for each student
- Get lab ready—turn on computers and projector
- Place handouts at each computer station needed for class
- Have pencils available, if needed

THE INSTRUCTION SESSION

- Welcome students to the Library
- Explain goals for session and introduce the Library's homepage
- Give instructions:
  - Divide class into five groups
  - Explain that each group will be assigned one section of the handout to complete, and will then teach the rest of the class the section they have completed.
- Groups will have about 15 minutes to complete their section before they teach
- The Librarian is available for questions, assistance, and encouragement
- During demonstration of a section, the rest of the class should follow along and fill out the applicable section of their handouts

ALLERGY WARNINGS

- Some groups need encouragement; walk around the room and talk to each group as they work
- Some students are shy, but quite a few ham it up when instructing their peers
- Check for errors and problem areas in each group's work; help them as necessary

CHEF'S NOTE

- This is the students' chance to show the class, the Professor, and the Librarian what marvelous and engaging teachers they are!
- Professors have given very positive feedback on this session

Library BINGO!

BINGO is a good one-shot activity to use when there is no other assignment associated with a class library visit or library instruction session.

Katherine O'Clair, Life Sciences Librarian, ASU Libraries, Tempe, Arizona, katherine.oclair@asu.edu

NUTRITION INFORMATION

This recipe is a great way to give students a basic introduction to the library using a variation of the traditional BINGO game. Students will practice using the library to find resources and information.

COOKING TIME

It is ideal for a session that is 45-60 minutes (could be shortened or extended to fit class session). The questions can be adapted for any course, but the activity is best for lower division undergraduate students with a class size less than fifty students.

ACRL INFORMATION DIETARY STANDARDS ADDRESSED

Standard Two: 2.1, 2.2, 2.3.

MAIN COOKING TECHNIQUE

Short demonstration, hands-on activity, point-of-need assistance and instruction

MAIN INGREDIENTS

- Computer workstations and Internet access for students
- Instructor workstation
- BINGO sheets
- BINGO questions
- Prizes

PREPARATION

1. Write BINGO questions based on the skills you would like to reinforce (e.g., finding an article, selecting a relevant database, retrieving a book from the shelf, etc.) and to fulfill your learning objectives. These questions can be general or subject-specific depending on the course.
2. Compile the correct answers to these BINGO questions on a separate sheet (answer key). You will use these to check the students' BINGO sheets.
3. Select several of these questions to demonstrate how to find the answer using the library's Web site and databases (these will be freebies for the students and will help keep them engaged during the demonstration).
4. Create five different BINGO sheets with different random numbers in the answer boxes using a spreadsheet program.
5. If desired, gather or purchase small and inexpensive prizes (chocolate bar, pen or highlighter with institution/library logo) for the winning team.

THE INSTRUCTION SESSION

1. When the students arrive in the library classroom, count students off so they are in groups of equal number (e.g., groups of two, three, four). Have them gather in their groups and get situated at the computer workstations and log in.
2. Pass out BINGO sheets for each student to complete. Do not pass out the questions yet. Each student must complete his or her own BINGO sheet.
3. Demonstrate the questions you selected that cover the extent of skills students will need to answer the BINGO questions. The students will get these as freebies on their BINGO sheets.
4. Pass out BINGO questions (do not pass these out ahead of time).
5. Students can begin working on BINGO questions as a group and filling the answers in the numbered boxes on the BINGO sheets that correspond to the question number. They have the option to ask for assistance from the librarian, but the exact answer should not be given.

6. When the first group has completed all the boxes on the BINGO sheet (or alternatively in a row), compare their answers with the answers key. If the group has any incorrect answers, they must go back and try to find the correct answer to those questions. The first group to have all members' sheets filled in with the correct answers wins. Second and third place can be awarded if desired. All students must complete the required questions and hand in the BINGO sheet.

Sample BINGO Questions:
- **What is the call number for the book The *Avian Brain* by Ronald Pearson?**
- **Do an online catalog search on a topic related to microbiology. Select a book from the list of results and go get it off the shelf. Be sure to write down the call number on the sheet and show the book to the librarian to get credit.**
- **How far back can you get Science in electronic format at the library?**

ALLERGY WARNINGS
Some particularly savvy students complete the down, across, or diagonal BINGO rows very quickly. One way to extend the activity is to have students complete the entire BINGO sheet.

All answers on the BINGO sheet must be correct, so the first group to finish is not necessarily the winner. Other groups should keep trying while the BINGO sheet is checked for the correct answers.

Most of the students take to this activity enthusiastically, but it definitely works better with traditional-age undergraduates who enjoy games.

CHEF'S NOTE
When students receive assignment points for the library activity, I have them complete a minimum number of questions whether they play BINGO or not. These questions are marked with an asterisk next to the number on the question sheet. These questions are more challenging and address the desired educational outcomes of the library instruction session.

This has been used for a general biology course and as an orientation to the library for students doing research projects. It is a fun way to give students the opportunity to practice using the library and gain skills.

	B	**I**	**N**	**G**	**O**
B	23	5	2	31	11
I	15	7	27	13	9
N	26	12	4	18	29
G	3	19	33	22	34
O	35	30	8	20	10

LC Face-Off

This recipe pits student teams against each other in a game format to test their knowledge of the LC call number system.

Jackie AlSaffar, Reference Librarian and Centers Liaison, Buena Vista University, alsaffarj@bvu.edu

NUTRITION INFORMATION

We typically use this after a general library training session for incoming employees or as a refresher for returning employees. The activity can be tailored to function as a second session for a general library orientation for students.

COOKING TIME

Cooking time is from 30-60 minutes depending on the skills of the students. Returning students, and upper-classmen, who have had more exposure to the LC system will zip through without a lot of difficulty or explanation. For that audience, however, we purposely make the slides tough.

ACRL INFORMATION DIETARY STANDARDS ADDRESSED

Standard One.

MAIN COOKING TECHNIQUE

Game

MAIN INGREDIENTS

- Instructor's station with projector
- PowerPoint software
- Whiteboard/blackboard

PREPARATION

Instructor prepares at least fifty slides/questions. Most slides will have two LC call numbers on them, side by side (written vertically as they would appear on the spine of a book). The call numbers on some will be in the correct order (as if they were sitting on the shelf). Others are not. Make them tricky and challenging! To keep things interesting, intersperse some short-answer slides regarding locations. For more variety, take screen shots of several records in the catalog. Again, ask them where the item would be located. This exercise ensures that students can translate what's on the screen into actually locating the item in the library.

THE INSTRUCTION SESSION

1. Students separate into two teams by counting off.

2. The first person in each line faces-off. A question is shown on screen. The first person to answer the question correctly scores a point. An incorrect answer gets a point erased. (Hint: On screens displaying two call numbers, the student will call out "yes" if the numbers are in correct shelf-order, and "no" if they are not. Also, the student must give a quick justification of the answer, such as: "Because .B39 shelves before .B6.") In the case of a tie, students will get another screen.

3. The second question goes to the second person in each line. Questions cycle through each person in the line. Then the first person on one team drops to the end of the line, and the students file forward, so as to be faced off with a different opponent each round.

4. When all questions are exhausted, or when time is up, points are tallied up.

5. The winning team wins token prizes (like college swag).

ALLERGY WARNINGS

It's important to stress to students that while this game favors the quick, in reality, it's much more important to be accurate.

CHEF'S NOTE

This interactive approach to testing students' knowledge has received positive feedback from students.

Stone Soup

The old fable of Stone Soup tells of a number of people providing some rather bizarre items for a communal cooking pot. This recipe will assist your students to make Stone Soup via a scavenger hunt.

Jennifer Hughes, Coastal Carolina University, jhughes@coastal.edu
Allison Faix, Coastal Carolina University, afaix@coastal.edu
Jamie Graham, NYU Health Sciences Libraries, Jamie.Graham@med.nyu.edu
Lisa Hartman, Coastal Carolina University, lhartman@coastal.edu

NUTRITION INFORMATION

This recipe was developed as a library instruction exercise for freshmen First Year Experience students, as a fun way to introduce students to the library's catalog and the physical layout of the building.

After a brief demonstration of search strategies using the online catalog, pairs of students are given unique clues with embedded keywords in the description that students must identify. Students navigate their way through the library collection in an effort to be the first team to return to the instruction room with their item for a prize.

COOKING TIME

Cooking time is 25 minutes. Serves twenty students

ACRL INFORMATION DIETARY STANDARDS ADDRESSED

Standard Two: 2.1, 2.2

MAIN COOKING TECHNIQUE

Mini-demonstrations, active small-group work, peer assistance, class discussion

MAIN INGREDIENTS

- Computers
- Pre-printed clues
- Prizes

PREPARATION

Creating and printing clues
Checking availability of the items

THE INSTRUCTION SESSION

1. Basic introduction of the online catalog and its limiting feature
2. Quick overview of scavenger hunt rules
3. Assignment of partners
4. Distribution of clues
5. Reward first successfully returning group with prizes
6. Peer-to-peer learning, students display found items and review their search strategies

ALLERGY WARNINGS

- Be prepared with prizes for ties
- Watch for lost students or unmotivated students
- Be prepared for items that are legitimately missing (disappeared between check and the class)

CHEF'S NOTE

Most students enjoy the challenge of competing against one another and the break in the class session. They are entertained by the interesting or unusual items that are brought back

Get Connected: A Challenge Board Game

Quia's Challenge Board Game provides an active methodology to generate interest in an introduction to the library.

Denise Pan, Associate Director of Technical Services and Assistant Professor at University of Colorado Denver, Auraria Library, denise.pan@ucdenver.edu

NUTRITION INFORMATION

The library's Get Connected session of the First Year Seminar (FYS) program at Johnson & Wales University Denver Campus, in most cases, was the students' introduction to the library. Playing this Challenge Board game provided a more interactive way to teach the library's rules than a traditional lecture.

COOKING TIME

Cooking time for this active recipe is 20 minutes. It serves approximately twenty-five students.

ACRL INFORMATION DIETARY STANDARDS ADDRESSED

Standard One: 1.1.

MAIN COOKING TECHNIQUE

Mini-demonstration, game

MAIN INGREDIENTS

- Computer with internet access for all students
- Instructor's station
- Subscription to Quia Web (1 year subscription for $49 at http://www.quia.com/subscription/)

PREPARATION

Identify five categories of topics and develop five questions with multiple-choice answers for each topic. Enter the questions and answers into Quia's Challenge Board game. Embed links to library Web pages that contain answers to the game's questions. The Get Connected Challenge Board can be viewed at http://www.quia.com/cb/209898.html.

In our Get Connected Challenge Board the five categories were the following:
1. All in the Numbers (fine rates, lending periods, and hours)
2. Check It Out (circulation policies)
3. Things That Begin with the Letter L (library policies)
4. That's IT (information technology)
5. Show Me the Books (resources and services)

All in the numbers	Check it out	Things that begin with the letter "l"	That's IT! (Information Technology)	Show me the books
100	100	100	100	100
200	200	200	200	200
300	300	300	300	300
400	400	400	400	400
500	500	500	500	500

THE INSTRUCTION SESSION

Quia's Challenge Board game can keep score for one or two players. This flexibility allows the game to be played by individuals, pairs, or two teams. How the class is divided depends on your eagerness to impersonate a game show host.
1. Demonstrate the interface.
2. Ask if there are any questions.
3. If playing in teams, divide up the class.

ALLERGY WARNINGS

Students generally take cues from other people in the room. If you are teaching with other instructors and/or faculty, ask them to participate and share in your enthusiasm for the game.

CHEF'S NOTE

Our main goal was to help our new students understand our expectations and rules. Even though they were brand new students, there was no need for them to feel lost or confused. We felt that if the students knew how things operated, they would be more inclined to visit the library.

Orientation Happytizer: The Library Welcomes New Freshmen

This recipe introduces first year students to the library facilities and services by providing a tour of the building and stacks.

Jenny Horton, Instructional Services Librarian, King College, Bristol, TN, jlhorton@king.edu

NUTRITION INFORMATION

Our First Year Experience (FYEX) course includes a meeting for an introduction to the library resources—physical, electronic and human. This meeting occurs within the first three weeks of classes, long before research assignments have been made and just in time for reserve readings.

COOKING TIME

Cooking time is 50 minutes. We will see up to twenty-five students each hour.

ACRL INFORMATION DIETARY STANDARDS ADDRESSED

Standard One: 1.2.
Standard Two: 2.3.

MAIN COOKING TECHNIQUE

Lecture, tour, and hands-on group activity

MAIN INGREDIENTS

- New students and the library
- Librarians to introduce various aspects of the library.

PREPARATION

Assignment sheets for the activity, with tasks requiring general information about the library and the use of library resources, guide the session. Librarians and staff agreed on points of interest in the library which should be included in the tour. With such a limited amount of time, the library staff agreed to limit the electronic resources overview to cover the library catalog and two databases.

INSTRUCTION SESSION

1. Divide the group in half. While one group attends an informational and interactive session on electronic resources in the computer lab, the other group tours the library, meets the staff, and hears a 2-3 minute story.
2. After 15 minutes, the groups switch places to receive the other half of the orientation.
3. For the remaining 20 minutes, the combined groups will work in teams of two to four answering questions on the Assignment Sheet based on the information provided in the tour and review of resources.

ALLERGY WARNINGS

Early morning classes were not as interested or as interactive as other sections. Fifty minutes is not nearly enough time to cover all that should be covered, but it's a great start to the year. Learning objectives must be prioritized and minimized. Several evaluation comments asked that we provide breakfast, candy, or food. We did provide free coffee!

CHEF'S NOTE

The story's purpose is to connect with the students on a human level. The story I used had nothing to do with college or the library, it spoke more about life. I told the story of *The Rainbow Fish* by Marcus Pfister. (Marcus Pfister. 1992. The Rainbow Fish. NY: North-South Books.)

Tailgate @ the Library (Everything's INSIDE the Library)

Invite students into the library during a fall home football game.

Nancy Noe, Instruction Coordinator, Auburn University, noenanc@auburn.edu

NUTRITION INFORMATION
This Fall Open House, held during a home football game, taps into a beloved campus tradition and introduces users to the physical layout of the library while emphasizing main service and help points. It also helps combat library anxiety.

COOKING TIME
Library Open House is targeted to incoming students, but all are invited. The largest attendance to date is 1800 plus.

ACRL INFORMATION DIETARY STANDARDS ADDRESSED
Standard Two: 2.3.

MAIN COOKING TECHNIQUE
Self-guided tour with prizes

MAIN INGREDIENTS
- Tailgate tents
- Giveaway items
- Food and drink
- School mascot, cheerleaders, marching band, other special guests
- Door prizes
- Decorations
- Advertising
- Personnel
- Inflatables

PREPARATION
- Steering committee begins work four months prior to event.

THE INSTRUCTION SESSION
1. As attendees enter the library they are given a ticket with at least two service points on each floor.
2. Tickets are stamped at each location
3. Each service point/station provides some kind of textual information/magnet/brochure, etc.
4. Participants completing ticket are eligible for a prize.

ALLERGY WARNINGS
The library will NOT be quiet. Faculty and staff will be involved for the majority of the day. A budget will be necessary.

CHEF'S NOTE
"Can you say football?" Who doesn't like a tailgate party? Participant reactions have been amazingly positive.

Go, Aubie the Tiger!

2. BASIC LIBRARY SKILLS

Boolean Simon Says

This active appetizer uses the children's game of Simon Says to teach students the basic concepts behind Boolean operators.

Janine Odlevak, Instructional Services Librarian, Spokane Community College, Spokane, WA, jodlevak@scc.spokane.edu

NUTRITION INFORMATION

Students have a difficult time understanding Boolean operators. The goal of this activity is to practice the concept of combining ideas using Boolean logic. The students themselves provide the examples.

COOKING TIME

Total cooking time is five minutes and the recipe serves a group of five or more (the more the better).

ACRL INFORMATION DIETARY STANDARDS ADDRESSED

Standard Two: 2.2.

MAIN COOKING TECHNIQUE

Group activity

MAIN INGREDIENTS

- Instructor station with computer and projector (This can be done verbally but it helps to have an instructor station.)
- PowerPoint presentation illustrating Boolean operators AND, OR, and NOT with accompanying Venn diagrams.

PREPARATION

Create PowerPoint slides or large paper charts of Boolean examples.

THE INSTRUCTION SESSION

Introduction. We are now going to practice using Boolean operators by playing Simon Says. I will be the researcher and you, the students, will act as my subjects.

1. **AND—First let's practice the concept AND.**

AND is used to narrow a search. (At this point, you may show a PPT slide or other type of Venn diagram depicting the AND concept.) Instruct students to:

1st Stand if you are a <u>college student</u>.
2nd Remain standing only if you are a <u>college student</u> AND you have <u>brown hair</u>.
3rd Remain standing now only if you are a <u>college student</u> AND have <u>brown hair</u> AND are <u>male</u>.

Point out that each of those left standing in the resulting search set has all three characteristics: <u>college student</u> and <u>brown hair</u> and <u>male</u>. Invite all students to be seated.

2. **OR—Now let's practice the concept OR.**

OR is used to broaden a search. OR gives you more. (Show a Venn diagram depicting the OR concept.) Instruct students to:

1st Stand if you are currently wearing <u>glasses</u>.
2nd Stand if you are currently wearing <u>glasses</u> OR <u>contacts</u>.
3rd Now stand if you are currently wearing <u>glasses</u> OR <u>contacts</u> OR if you <u>ever</u> wear glasses or contacts (to drive or read).

Point out that those now standing are your set of people who require some type of vision correction. Invite all students to be seated again.

3. NOT—Lastly we'll practice the concept NOT.

NOT is used to exclude a search concept. It's easy to understand, but harder to act out; let's try it. (Show a Venn diagram depicting the NOT concept.) Instruct students to:

1st   Stand if you are a <u>college student</u>.
2nd   Now remain standing only if you are college student who is <u>NOT</u> <u>male</u>.

Explain that you started with a large set of <u>college students</u> and then removed the set of all the <u>males</u>, leaving only the females remaining.

Wrap-up. Now that they have a general idea of how the Boolean Operators work, invite students to be seated one last time and thank them for acting as your subjects.

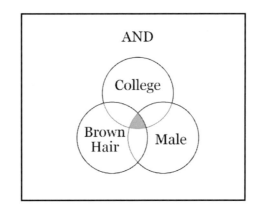

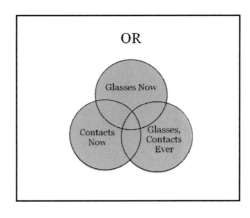

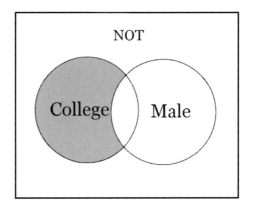

ALLERGY WARNINGS

Be aware of your students' physical capabilities when asking them to respond to your prompts. If students have limited mobility, you may need to require another form of response instead of standing: hand-raising, electronic response devices, holding up a sheet of colored paper, etc.

CHEF'S NOTE

In addition to reinforcing the Boolean operators concept, this activity can provide an on-task opportunity for students to get up and move a bit during an instruction session. If the examples given here don't suit your population, adapt the search criteria so that each audience member has at least one opportunity to respond. The NOT activity (where students remain standing if they are NOT male) always causes a chuckle and bit of chatter as students of the wrong gender sit or remain standing in error—a nice way to lighten the mood of a class absorbed in deep concentration.

Boolean a la Chinese Menu

This appetizer compares ordering a meal from a Chinese menu to creating search strings using Boolean connectors.

Dr. Sara Rofofsky Marcus, Kurt R. Schmeller Library, Queensborough Community College, smmarcus@qcc.cuny.edu

NUTRITION INFORMATION

This is a general introduction to the use of Boolean search strategies. The goal is to introduce the concept of creating a complex search statement in a way that is similar to choosing from a Chinese menu.

COOKING TIME

Cooking time is one hour maximum. Serving size varies.

ACRL INFORMATION DIETARY STANDARDS ADDRESSED

Standard One: 1.1.
Standard Two: 2.2.

MAIN COOKING TECHNIQUE

Demonstration, discussion, hands-on practice

MAIN INGREDIENTS

- SMART board or projector with Internet-ready computer
- One computer per student or per student group
- Copies of blank Boolean Tables for student use

PREPARATION

- Copy blank Boolean Tables for student use
- Provide students with thesauri
- Obtain or recreate samples of the Chinese menu which demonstrates selecting one item from column A and another from column B, etc.

THE INSTRUCTION SESSION

- Share the Chinese menu with students and demonstrate ordering a meal. This helps give a real life situation to the use of Boolean logic.
- Have students work on identifying key concepts in a research question. Begin with your own topic and determine key concepts that might appear. As students suggest concepts, fill in your own Boolean Table. Explain to students that the first term used for a key concept becomes a keyword and other terms that mean the same become synonyms. Show how the columns and rows demonstrate AND or OR.

ALLERGY WARNINGS

Be prepared with topics if students forget. Have thesauri ready. Students may not have ordered from a Chinese menu before so be sure to have examples

CHEF'S NOTE

After the first implementation of this assignment, I realized that I needed to bring sample menus as some students were not familiar with Chinese menus. Filled-out sample Boolean Tables would greatly enhance this session, as would using colors to help students align portions of the examples.

	Chinese Menu	
	Choose One from each column	
SOUP	MEAT	VEGETABLES
S1—Hot & Sour	M1—Orange Beef	V1—Broccoli
S2—Egg Drop	M2—Sweet & Sour Pork	V2—Mushrooms

Catalogs, Databases, and Firefighters! Oh My!

This recipe uses a number of active teaching techniques to introduce students to the library catalog, WorldCat, and Academic Search Premier.

Michelle Price, St. John Fisher College, mprice@sjfc

NUTRITION INFORMATION

Since some of the students were writing about different careers, I chose firefighters as a general topic. Using a worksheet, students began by finding books on firefighters. Then in pairs, students were asked to create a short skit about a person looking for a book in the library. Finally students were asked to draw a picture of a library in which everything was free.

COOKING TIME

Cooking time is 80 minutes. Serves twenty first-year students.

ACRL INFORMATION DIETARY STANDARDS ADDRESSED

Standard Two: 2.1, 2.3.
Standard Four: 4.1.
Standard Five: 5.1.

MAIN COOKING TECHNIQUE

Worksheets, skits, discussion groups, drawings

MAIN INGREDIENTS

- Worksheets
- Dry-erase boards and markers, (or paper and markers)
- Student computers

PREPARATION

Make sure introductory worksheets are available. Markers should be available at each whiteboard.

THE INSTRUCTION SESSION

1. **Worksheet on finding books**
   a. Students individually look up a book on firefighting in the catalog.
   b. Answer questions about the book using the book record.
   c. Repeat the process in WorldCat.
2. **Book finding skits**
   In pairs, students create and enact a skit about two people looking for a book.
3. **Essential questions discussion**
   a. Why are some things free and some things fee? What would the library look like if all information were free?
   b. Students work in small discussion groups to think about the two questions.
4. **Pictures of free libraries**
   a. Then they draw a picture of what a college library would look like if all information were free.
   b. Student groups present their future library and explain why certain features are present or absent.

5. **Worksheet on finding articles**
   They complete handout about different ways to limit a search in Academic Search Premier.

ALLERGY WARNINGS

- Not every group will want to perform their skit, but it still works out okay if only one group volunteers.
- You may need to cue students to add more information to their picture.

CHEF'S NOTE

I did this lesson with two different English Composition classes and tumbleweeds showed up in both classes. The drawings could have been a catalyst for lots of other discussions, such as information ownership as power, the digital divide, mob mentality, and funding.

The Coffee Can Appetizer

A series of coffee cans represent various databases. Each is filled with objects which give clues as to the actual database's contents. Teams of students explore each can and report to the whole group.

Virginia L. Cairns, Head of Reference and Instruction, Lupton Library, U. of Tennessee, Chattanooga, virginia-cairns@utc.edu

NUTRITION INFORMATION

This activity is excellent as a class opener for First Year Composition students. This activity will help beginning college students understand the following concepts:

- The difference between library databases and the internet
- The types of content available in library databases
- The difference between broad multi-subject databases and discipline-specific databases

COOKING TIME

Cooking time is between 10 and 15 minutes. Ideally, serves fifteen people in order to make the groups large enough to generate lively interaction and discussion.

ACRL INFORMATION DIETARY STANDARDS ADDRESSED

Standard Two.
Standard Three.

MAIN COOKING TECHNIQUE

Appetizer, hands-on group activity, group discussion

MAIN INGREDIENTS

The coffee cans should be of differing sizes to represent the concept that databases come in different sizes. The larger cans indicate larger databases, etc. They should also be painted or decorated with the logos of different database products. We use:

- Academic OneFile (a large blue can)
- LexisNexis (a large red can)
- PsycINFO (a medium-sized green can)
- ARTstor (a very small brown can)
- Google (a large, white, lidded 5-gallon paint bucket)

Inside each can are collections of colorful laminated cards describing items that can be found in that particular product.

- Visual items—the actual images of journal and magazine covers contained in the database
- Factual information items—for example, "Full text of the articles from over 2,600 professional business and trade journals."
- Textual items—citations and full text to illustrate the concept that not all articles in all databases are full text.

- The Google trash can has many items inside it, including cards for things like PORN (a very large black and white sign), shopping sites, American Idol.com, ESPN.com, Wikipedia, Lindsay Lohan's picture, etc. There is also a toy car inside (labeled for sale on eBay). Students LOVE to play with the car.

In addition to the cans, there should also be large, colored cards with research questions on them—one card that matches with the content for each database.

PREPARATION

Before class, simply line up the cans on a table or even on the floor in front of the classroom. Have the question cards at the podium.

THE INSTRUCTION SESSION

1. Hand each group a can and have them move to a corner of the room.
2. Instruct the groups to explore the contents of their cans, keeping in mind that each can represents a different resource they could use for locating material for their assignments. Give the groups 2 or 3 minutes to explore and discuss among themselves.
3. Ask each group to tell the class about their can. Begin with the larger databases.
4. Prompt them for specifics about the contents of the can that you know to be relevant to their research needs For example, if the group that has the LexisNexis can doesn't mention the newspaper articles in their can, ask, "Did you find any news sources in your can?"

5. Save the Google group for last. They will have a particularly fun time showing off what they found in their can (especially the toy car). There is also one textual card in the Google can that has a price tag attached to it. Ask them if they have ever encountered a site asking for their credit card number in order to download an article. MANY have had this experience. Use this opportunity to emphasize that some content you find in Google comes at a price, but the same content can sometimes be had for free through the library Web site. This helps cement the idea that the resources provided through the library website are costly and valuable. (Our Google can example is an APA article that can be found in PsycINFO.)
6. After all the cans have been introduced, then take your question cards from the podium and read them aloud one by one. Ask the students to guess which database would be used to answer that question. They usually guess very quickly and by the time the activity concludes, students are very comfortable with the concept of what a library database is and why they should not use Google for a term paper.

ALLERGY WARNINGS

One thing to watch out for is losing control of the class when the Google bucket gets introduced. Sometimes it's necessary to insist they quiet down so the activity can continue. There is sometimes quite a bit of laughing and rowdiness, especially with the porn sign and the toy car.

CHEF'S NOTE

At UTC, we've found that we absolutely adore hands-on activities like this one. Traditional lecture classes sometimes never give the librarian a chance to develop a good back-and-forth conversation with the students. Now, we begin all of our First Year Composition classes with this activity which starts the students of with an enjoyable activity, which sets the tone for the rest of the session.

Database Cafe

A seat in this cafe will provide new students with a banquet of information about basic searching in databases.

Lai Kei Pang, Manukau Institute of Technology, Auckland, New Zealand, l.pang@auckland.ac.nz; Musarrat Begum, Manukau Institute of Technology, Auckland, New Zealand, m.begum@massey.ac.nz

NUTRITION INFORMATION
Database Cafe is a collaborative cooking session in which students learn the types of resources which can be retrieved from databases, plus how to retrieve those resources. Students are given some ingredients (e.g. database name, electronic folders) and they have to add their own (search terms) to prepare a dish as a group.

COOKING TIME
Cooking time is two-hours for students new to EBSCOhost databases and re-searching articles on a particular topic in the Social Sciences. Serving size is twenty students.

ACRL INFORMATION DIETARY STANDARDS ADDRESSED
Standard One: 1.1, 1.2.
Standard Two: 2.2, 2.4, 2.5.
Standard Four: 4.1.

MAIN COOKING TECHNIQUE
Hands-on, demonstration, small groups, instructions on activity sheet

MAIN INGREDIENTS
- Data projector
- Computer for each participant
- Internet access to databases
- Printer
- Pen and paper

PREPARATION
Make sure students have a research topic ready. An electronic folder needs to be created on EBSCOhost for each group, including a username and password.

THE INSTRUCTION SESSION
1. **Demonstration and explanation of activity—10 minutes.**
   - Librarian explains citation details and how to use EBSCOhost databases to retrieve articles; brief demonstration.

2. ***Activity I: Who are the blue-ribbon chefs? 15 minutes.***
   - Students are each given five articles to retrieve; each article has some ingredients missing (e.g. the title, the author, the publication date, etc.)
   - Students find the missing ingredients by retrieving the articles from the databases.
   - Students fill in the missing details on the sheet for Activity 1. The first three students who find all the missing ingredients get a prize for being the blue-ribbon chefs.

3. ***Activity II, Part 1: Where are the ingredients from? 65 minutes.***
   Students form into groups of four to do the following collaborative cooking.
   A. Recipe books (databases) given—5 minutes.
      - Each group has the same research topic but is assigned a different EBSCOhost database (academic, multi-disciplinary, popular, newspaper, New Zealand / Australia, or subject specific).
   B. Cooking five dishes (retrieving five articles)—20 minutes.
      - Members in each group discuss the search concepts to use. Each group carries out research using their own search words. Each group needs to find five articles and put them in the group's EBSCOhost electronic folder.

C. Explaining the recipe books (databases) and the chefs' input (search words used)—20 minutes.
   - When all the groups have finished the task, one representative from each group explains briefly to the whole class regarding which database they were assigned. The representative also writes the group's search words on the white board.
D. Tasting the dishes (articles)—20 minutes.
   - The librarian opens the electronic folders one-by-one using the data projector so that all the students can see the articles in each folder. Each student looks at the articles in each of the folders and decides from which database each folder comes from. Each folder should contain articles from one database.
E. Which recipe books (databases) are the dishes (articles) from?
   - Each student identifies on the activity sheet from which database each folder (of articles) is retrieved. There is one score for each correct identification. Whoever gets all correct will be given a prize for being the blue-ribbon food taster.

4. ***Activity II, Part 2: Evaluation—10 minutes.***
   - Students discuss their answers (why they got them wrong).
   - Students discuss the search terms the other groups used.

ALLERGY WARNINGS
Are you allergic to databases? This activity could have healing effects. Students were at different levels of computer skills, so they were allowed to retrieve as many citations as they could within the time limit.

CHEF'S NOTE
   - Two hours recommended. You should include the last activity to give the students a sense of achievement.
   - Students were engaged with the group activity (Activity II) because they could each contribute their strengths (computer, search, presentation, or leadership skills).
   - We recommend two librarians to conduct the session, to ensure that prompt help is given when needed.

Krafting Keywords from Topics

Using a worksheet to help students transform keywords into a search statement.

Justine Martin, Library Instruction Coordinator, Minnesota State University, Mankato, justine.martin@mnsu.edu

NUTRITION INFORMATION

This activity, using an information search worksheet, guides students through a basic, yet effective process of breaking down a research topic into a keyword search. The students test their newly created search in a database, and then modify the keywords based on the initial results. It complements classes in which students have individual research topics, although example topics can also be distributed to practice the process.

COOKING TIME

Cooking time is 20-30 minutes and serves twenty-five first-year students.

ACRL INFORMATION DIETARY STANDARDS ADDRESSED

Standard One: 1.1.
Standard Two: 2.2, 2.4.
Standard Four: 4.2.

MAIN COOKING TECHNIQUE

Hands-on experiential learning, worksheet

MAIN INGREDIENTS

- Instructor workstation
- Computer and internet access
- Document camera for paper worksheet (optional)
- Information search worksheet

PREPARATION

Contact the course instructor to see if students will have their research topics selected by the time of the library session. Print copies of the information search worksheet.

THE INSTRUCTION SESSION

1. Hand out the worksheet and ask students to have a pen/pencil ready.
2. Direct students to write down their topic in phrase or sentence form in section 1.
3. Have students circle descriptive words while crossing out pronouns, definite and indefinite articles, and prepositions.
4. Students should write their descriptive words in section 2 of the worksheet.
5. Show students how to place the Boolean operator AND between the words. Explain how AND is a narrowing tool.
6. Referring to section 3, instruct students to test their search in a journal database or library catalog. Depending on the database, show students how to format their search within search box areas.
7. After students conduct their search, ask about their results. Do the results match their topic? Did they find too many results or too few?
8. Provide hands-on practice time for the class, while working with individual students to address their specific search dilemmas.

Information Search Worksheet

LIBRARY SERVICES
lib.mnsu.edu

1 Your Research Topic

What are the key words or phrases in your research topic? Write the words in section 2.

Write Your Topic Here:_____

Then circle the important words and cross out the other words

Example: ~~Should~~ (Wikipedia) ~~be used as a~~ (source) ~~of~~ (information?)

| Circle important words or phrases that best describes your topic | Avoid using vague or non-descriptive words like **the, it, in, used, at.** |

Place the circled words in the box in section 2.

2 Transforming Keywords into a Search Statement

Connect your keywords or phrases with AND

Example using **AND**	Your new search statement connected with **AND**	Why use **AND**?
wikipedia **and** source **and** information		**AND** focuses your search by requiring all words be present in the information retrieved

3 Test Your Search Statement

Test your search in a library database on the Library Services website at lib.mnsu.edu:

For books: use the **Books** quick search box on the center of the page	*For journals*, go to **Article Databases A-Z** and select **Academic Search Premier**
ONE box Searching: Type AND between your search words in one long string	THREE box Searching: Place each keyword or phrase in a box. **AND** is automatically placed in between the boxes.
Search for: wikipedia and source and information	**Find:** source / and wikipedia / and information

ALLERGY WARNINGS
This activity is most effective when students have their own research topics. Students have greater intrinsic motivation to implement the worksheet's strategies when they need to gather literature for an assignment. Otherwise, a library instructor can give example topics to students. If example topics are distributed, reduce the amount of hands-on time since students will not use the information found during the session for a future assignment.

CHEF'S NOTE
This activity is an effective way to integrate search strategies such as Boolean operators into a student's research process. I use this activity after introducing the library Web site, but before demonstrating databases. I focus the students' attention on the worksheet and work with them to implement the strategies in this activity to locate relevant sources. Most students are grateful to learn quick techniques prior to their information search.

Keyword Reduction Sauce

This recipe assists students to reduce thesis statements into keywords.

Robert S. Nelson, Library Instruction Coordinator, College of Staten Island, CUNY, nelsonr@mail.csi.cuny.edu

NUTRITION INFORMATION

The purpose of this activity is to add flavor and spice to database searches through the liberal application of effectively selected keywords. Allowing students to reduce their thesis statements into a select set of keywords, helps to focus their database searching and permits them to be more critical in their article selection.

COOKING TIME

This recipe feeds twenty to thirty undergraduates and needs to simmer for 90 to 120 minutes.

ACRL INFORMATION DIETARY STANDARDS ADDRESSED

Standard Two: 2.2, 2.3, 2.4.

MAIN COOKING TECHNIQUE

Demonstration, group discussion

MAIN INGREDIENTS

- Keyword Worksheet
- Student access to online databases
- Instructor's Station

PREPARATION

- Select a handful of ripe and healthy thesis statements. Hint: Using locally grown statements (developed by a librarian/professorial cooperative) is strongly encouraged.
- Steep all thesis statements in a solution of critical analysis. As the librarian, you should be able to extract three to four useful keywords from each statement.
- Using a pinch of keywords, apply to the database of choice to test for efficacy.
- Once you have taste-tested the keywords, arrange them on a handout with space to allow students to identify the keywords and write them down.
- Shake (print) until the correct amount is yielded.

THE INSTRUCTION SESSION

1. Gather students in a classroom or computer lab.
   a. They may work in groups if need be.
   b. Results and cooking time may vary depending on size and composure of groups.
2. Briefly explain the importance of reducing thesis statements into keywords.
   a. Use an example of a complex thesis statement that can be reduced to several words.
   b. Mention concepts such as indexing and controlled vocabulary to assist in the overall cooking time.
   c. Emphasize the efficiency and tastiness of creating key words prior to searching. If time permits, explain how this process can aid in selecting articles.
   d. Using more than 10 minutes to complete this process will burn the students' attention span to a crisp and unusable crust. 2-5 minute is the optimal time to introduce the activity.
3. Allow students 15-20 minutes to reduce several statements into keywords. Once again, the number of statements and time allotted may vary depending on group sizes and composure.
4. Once the appropriate time has elapsed, lower flame and open for discussion.
   a. Allowing the class to cool before adding the database search is crucial so as not to overpower the class with tasks.

b. Discuss the reduction process and ask students to share results. If electronic whiteboards or classroom control software are present, they may be used.
5. Prepare students to add reductions by demonstrating access to several library databases.
   a. Pay very close attention to time, more than 10 minutes of this and you will burn their attention span.
   b. Instruct students to add newly reduced keywords to the database and let simmer for 20-30 minutes.
6. While simmering, walk around the classroom and sample the results, adding a pinch of advice or direction to intensify the learning. But be careful not to overpower the discussion or its taste will be washed out.
7. Once the time has elapsed, you may wish to invite a taste test.
   a. Have the students share their successes and failures with the group.
   b. Moderate a discussion of why the reduction of the thesis statement is dependant on personal taste.
   c. Highlight how different databases yield different results even when the ingredients are similar.

ALLERGY WARNINGS

Depending on class size and structure, reductions may take longer. Adjustments should be made after consulting with professor. Null results will be met with agitation by the students. Working with them to reexamine their keyword set is important.

CHEF'S NOTE

Slow food has become a theme in trendy restaurants lately. I would like to start a Slow Searching trend. Students are often too goal-oriented when attending library sessions, I like to slow down the pace a bit and emphasize process over results. By teaching them to properly keyword a thesis statement, you're not only improving their searching skills, but focusing them on the most important aspects of their topic. If they are able to effectively keyword a complex topic, then they are capable of higher levels of critical thinking too. For me, the ability to keyword is the pathway to true critical thinking.

Taming the Taboo

This recipe requires that students work in groups to brainstorm and use keywords to search for predetermined topics. The trick is—it's TABOO to use the words provided. Students must come up with synonyms.

Jason Dupree, Head of Public Services and Assistant Professor, Southwestern Oklahoma State University, Weatherford, OK, jason.dupree@swosu.edu

NUTRITION INFORMATION

Our library introduces students to academic-level research in a four-part information literacy series held in the library. This recipe takes place during the third session as students examine article databases. With this activity students are encouraged to explore databases with various search strategies to accomplish a specific research goal. Composition students are asked to select a topic for a three to five page research paper assignment. These papers focus on the formulation of well-constructed arguments, thoughtful research, and correctly formatted bibliographies.

COOKING TIME

Cooking time is 50-75 minutes. Serves Freshmen or Sophomore classes of twenty to thirty students.

ACRL INFORMATION DIETARY STANDARDS ADDRESSED

Standard One: 1.1, 1.2, 1.3, 1.4.
Standard Two: 2.2, 2.4.
Standard Three: 3.3, 3.6.

MAIN COOKING TECHNIQUE

Small-group work, peer assistance

MAIN INGREDIENTS

- Computer access for all students.
- An article database that provides a wide range of topics, such as, EBSCOHost Academic Search Complete.
- An instructor's station with projector.
- Dry-erase board/markers.

PREPARATION

Pre-select six topics. Divide the dry-erase board into six equal areas. The title of each topic will be placed at the top of each section. Underneath the topic header, write the numbers one through three for groups to list their answers.

THE INSTRUCTION SESSION

1. Demonstration on the use of an article database. Remind students of the importance of searching techniques (10 minutes).
2. Break class into six groups (four to six students in each).
   a. Group 1 will be assigned the topic "corporate social responsibility."
   b. Group 2 will be assigned the topic "death penalty for teens."
   c. Group 3 will be assigned the topic "social networking Web sites."
   d. Group 4 will be assigned the topic "global warming and pollution."
   e. Group 5 will be assigned the topic "prescription drugs and obesity."
   f. Group 6 will be assigned the topic "affirmative action in the workplace."
3. Give students the instructions regarding how the exercise is to be completed (1-2 minutes).
   a. Each group will research their assigned topic within an article database.

b. The words provided cannot be used in the database search—it's taboo! Groups will need to determine synonyms and/or related terms to achieve the proper results.

c. Once groups have determined a successful search strategy, they must provide answers to the following three questions:

   i. What related terms did you come up with?

   ii. How did you construct your search strategy?

   iii. How many results did you find?

d. A designated recorder will post their answers on the dry-erase board.

4. Clarify any misunderstanding or answer any questions.

5. When all groups have recorded their findings, the concluding dialogue will open a discussion of keyword generation, search strategy revision, and information satisfaction.

ALLERGY WARNINGS

Students will need to be encouraged to think outside the box.

CHEF'S NOTE

I find this to be a refreshing approach to the traditional database show-and-tell. Also, this exercise provides a nice review of searching techniques. The preparation of this exercise takes longer than the actual activity does in the classroom. We realize a focus must be maintained on the principles of conducting research; however, to challenge the students to learn the process of critical thinking, the placement of a barrier in their research task helps them explore the possible choices available to them. I've been approached by several teaching faculty who approve of this activity as a teaching tool.

Why Won't the Database Answer My Question?

This recipe is a balance of small group work and large group discussion. Students work on creating search strategies.

Lyda Ellis, Instruction Librarian and Assistant Professor, University of Northern Colorado, Greeley, CO, lyda.ellis@unco.edu

NUTRITION INFORMATION

Many freshmen at the University of Northern Colorado get their first introduction to subscription databases during their first semester. These students are used to searching Google and other search engines, but are not familiar with the precision needed to conduct effective searches in a library database. This recipe will work for classes coming into the library for any subject. This would be useful for a school media center if there are an adequate number of computers.

COOKING TIME

Serves a room full of college freshmen. Cooking time is 60 to 75 minutes.

ACRL INFORMATION DIETARY STANDARDS ADDRESSED

Standard Two: 2.2, 2.4.
Standard Four: 4.2.

MAIN COOKING TECHNIQUE

Mini-discussions with group participation, small-group work in computer lab, hands-on discussion session

MAIN INGREDIENTS

Computer Access for all students
Instructor station with projector
Thesaurus for each group
White Board with markers (flip chart would work)

PREPARATION

Develop a research question, typically something the students are interested in, such as, "What is the impact of the internet on the music industry?" This question is written on the board before the students enter class. If possible, have the question covered with the projector screen or a sheet of long paper.

THE INSTRUCTION SESSION

1. Introduction
   a. Have students type a question into the Academic Search Premier basic search box (such as "Do Cigarettes Cause Cancer?); students can follow along or just watch the screen.
   b. Ask the students how many results they think the database will retrieve. Let the students call out the numbers; this works best if you can make it like an auction—"I've got 100 over here, 50 over here, he says 15,000." Select search—this will return zero results. (Act surprised too!!)
   c. Ask the students why the database gave us no results. Discuss the difference between a subscription database and Google. Most of the time one or two students will say that the question is too specific or that there are too many words. These answers will typically move you right into the database vs. Google talk.
   d. Discuss using keywords only in the database, rather than natural language queries.
2. Group work
   a. Ask students to move into small groups. Uncover the research question on the board.
   b. Ask students which words of our search question we would leave off if we wanted to find articles in the database on the topic. Erase the words the students call out.
   c. Have students come up with two synonyms for each of the keywords left on the board using a thesaurus. (They can use dictionary.com since

they have computer access.)

d. Walk around to each group to see progress and discuss possible keywords.

e. Ask each group to give their best synonym for each keyword.

3. Discussion

a. Discuss the Search Strategy concept and introduce Boolean Operators. Discuss Boolean Operators as a way that you talk to the database—a mathematical equation with words!!

4. Group Work

a. Have each group create search strategies using their keywords and two Boolean Operators.

5. Discussion

a. Have one member of each group come to the board and write the group's search strategy.

b. Have the class vote on the best search strategy on the board.

c. Have each student type the search strategy into the database to see which actually finds the best results.

6. Discussion

a. Discuss the importance of creating lists of synonyms.

b. Discuss refining the search using limiters, such as date, full text, and peer reviewed.

c. Discuss Popular vs. Scholarly articles

7. Review

a. Have students get back in groups while the instructor writes another question on the board. Have students create a search strategy using keywords and Boolean operators. The students are required to find one scholarly article on the topic. This reviews search strategies, Boolean operators, and limiters.

ALLERGY WARNINGS

This session can get loud! Students usually think up two or three keywords that are not correct, but sound funny when they say them out loud. You must be able to reign in the discussion. Some students will struggle with finding the scholarly article. While showing the limiter for Peer Reviewed articles, it is also good to go over the characteristics of scholarly research.

CHEF'S NOTE

I love teaching this session because it is not like a typical library session. There is a discussion rather than a lecture and there are hands-on activities rather than demonstrations by the librarian. I have never had a student not get involved! Since I've been introducing databases this way I have found students get very energetic about the session. Students gain a better understanding of putting together a search strategy because they are required to think instead of merely listen.

The best part is the flexibility of this activity! You can use the same activity for upper division classes by doing a short review of Boolean Operators and search strategies, and then taking the searches into more specialized databases such as JSTOR. This session also works well for subject specific sections. You can tailor the research questions to a major and use subject specific databases. This is nice because the students can use the technical language of the discipline when searching.

This is a great session for the freshmen and the senior!

Chocolate Upside-down Research Process

"This is Henry. He is my nine month old son. Henry is a genius..."

Mary Francis, Reference/Instruction Librarian, Dakota State University, mary.francis@dsu.edu

NUTRITION INFORMATION

"...He is going to write a research paper on the stereotypes placed on infants in the popular media. Unfortunately, he has never written a research paper before and has no idea of the process involved. You need to explain the process to him." This Chocolate Upside-down Research Process puts the hard work of thinking through the research process on the shoulders of the student chefs.

COOKING TIME

Cooking time is 50 minutes at 350 degrees and can be used for general research across all disciplines—all taste buds. Serves approximately twenty-five students, four to five per serving in an introductory English composition class.

ACRL INFORMATION DIETARY STANDARDS ADDRESSED

Standard One: 1.1, 1.4.
Standard Two: 2:2.
Standard Three: 3.6.
Standard Four: 4.1.

MAIN COOKING TECHNIQUE

Small group work, oral presentation, focused discussion

MAIN INGREDIENTS

- Projector with faculty station or whiteboard

PREPARATION

Optional—Research Process Worksheet to be completed by students as they conduct their research. Worksheet created by Risë Smith, Digital Design & Access Librarian

THE INSTRUCTION SESSION

1. Mix students together in several small bowls.
2. Provide them with the following situation: This is Henry (picture of baby is shown). He is my nine month old son. (Not all librarians will have a toddler to use as an example, so I recommend using a photo of a pet dog, cat, etc. This provides a personal touch to the session and makes the librarian more approachable and human.) Henry is a genius and is going to write a research paper on the stereotypes placed on infants in the popular media. Unfortunately, he has never written a research paper before and has no idea of the process involved. You need to explain the process to him. You will need to be very detailed and specific as this is completely new to him. After your group has developed a research process to share with Henry, you will come to the front of the class and share it with everyone else. As you are preparing your process, think of the steps that you use when you conduct research and tips on what works well.

3. Allow the groups to beat on medium speed for 10 minutes or until stiff peaks form.
4. The groups are then asked to come to the front and share their processes either by typing their steps on the faculty station or by writing on the whiteboard.
5. Discuss their steps including topics such as: what worked, how long the process took, why they included each step, etc.
6. Present the library's research process and worksheet.
7. Fold their steps into the steps offered by the library worksheet, showing how the integrity of all the ingredients is maintained during the incorporation.
8. Follow with a discussion of the feelings they will experience during the process (as per Carol Kuhlthau's Information Search Process).
9. Summarize session so that the knife of questions inserted into the middle comes out clean.

Kuhlthau, Carol Collier. Teaching the Library Research Process. Metuchen, N.J.: Scarecrow Press, 1994.

ALLERGY WARNINGS

Should your soufflé fall and you have trouble getting participation in the discussion, make sure you have a backup plan to re-connect the class. For example, choose one student and have them go through the research process with you—have them share their topic, help them to focus it, determine where they will look for information, etc. asking the rest of the class for input along the way.

CHEF'S NOTE

- Make the students come to the front to present.
- The students do have a prior understanding/knowledge of the research process as explained by the library. The real issue is the fact that they do not follow their own advice.
- Some groups have included steps such as, "Wait until the night before the paper is due." While adding a pinch of laughter, statements such as these are the start of great discussion points by asking what happens when you procrastinate and what steps are then cut out in order to get the paper done.
- Yet within all of the complexity of research, it is also a process. Just as in the case of the writing process, students should be given a format to follow to aid them as they find the information necessary for research in its many forms.

Parsley, Sage, Rosemary, and Find: A Five-Course Banquet

This recipe is for a luscious five-course banquet—served one course at a time.

Carol Howe, Immaculata University, chowe@immaculata.edu

NUTRITION INFORMATION
Each of five student dining groups is responsible for a preparing and presenting a course. One bountiful course follows another until students have learned the basics of developing and following through on a database search strategy as an initial step in the research process. This session is intended for students who are familiar with computers and surfing the Web but have not had formal information research instruction.

COOKING TIME
Cooking time is 45 to 60 minutes. Serves ten to twenty undergraduates or adult continuing education students.

ACRL INFORMATION DIETARY STANDARDS ADDRESSED
Standard One: 1.1.
Standard Two: 2.2, 2.4.
Standard Three: 3.7.

MAIN COOKING TECHNIQUE
Demonstration, small-group work, peer-assistance, presentations

MAIN INGREDIENTS
- Whiteboard with markers and erasers
- Computer and projector with screen
- Flip chart (only if the screen blocks the board when lowered)

PREPARATION
The only preparation needed is to create two scholarly research questions: one to demonstrate and one to give to the students.

THE INSTRUCTION SESSION
1. Setting the Table (10 minutes)
Instructor demonstrates a search in a database appropriate to the research question chosen, e.g., "Why are today's youth abusing prescription drugs?" Instructor should demonstrate the following:
- Breaking the topic down into its main concepts
- Brainstorming synonyms for the main concepts
- Connecting search terms with Boolean operators
- Applying truncation to search terms
- Applying limits to the search

2. Hors d'oeuvres (10 minutes)
- Instructor gives the class a research question: e.g., "How does listening to violent music lyrics affect teens?"
- Instructor divides the class into small groups
- Each group is asked to determine the topic's three main concepts
- Each group discusses their findings with the class, and a consensus is reached

3. The Five-Course Banquet (25 minutes)
1st Course: Hearty alphabet soup (i.e., vocabulary stew)
Group 1 comes up with synonyms, acronyms, and variant spellings for each of the three main concepts and writes them on the board.

2nd Course: Boolean salad with ((goat cheese OR feta cheese) AND vinaigrette dressing)

<u>Group 2</u> adds the Boolean operators AND & OR to join all the search terms provided by Group 1.

3rd Course: Word-stems topped with sliced almonds

<u>Group 3</u> applies truncation to the search terms on the board (using erasers if necessary!).

- The group explains what word variations each instance of truncation will find.

4th Course: Chicken in pan-reduced garlic sauce (save room for dessert—limit yourself!)

<u>Group 4</u> suggests ways to limit the search

e.g., Should you search for your words in the entire text or just in the title, abstract, or other field? Do you only want scholarly articles or do you want to include newspaper and popular magazine articles? Do you want recent articles or doesn't it matter how old the articles are?

5th Course: Everything-but-the-kitchen-sink brownie sundae

<u>Group 5</u> puts it all together and demonstrates the search in an appropriate database.

- Group elicits feedback from the class about how to revise the search if desired results are not obtained.

ALLERGY WARNINGS

- Make sure the research questions you choose have ample results.
- While one group works on the task at hand, keep other groups busy brainstorming ideas of their own. Groups can help each other during the presentation phase!
- This activity has the potential to take longer than expected if conversations start. Keep students focused.
- Students may come up with many more synonyms than you imagined. Use this as a teaching opportunity to explain why some search terms may cause unexpected results, e.g., *rap** would not only find *rap music* but also *rapid* and *rapport*.

CHEF'S NOTE

- Students are forced to break down the search strategy into manageable chunks.
- Students participate in active learning which enhances their memory of the concepts covered.
- This activity gives both the instructor and students ample opportunity to interact with one another and have fun with the research process.

They Are Already Experts

True to their claim, students can usually Google information on any topic in less than 10 seconds.

Sara Miller, Michigan State University, smiller@mail.lib.msu.edu

NUTRITION INFORMATION

Students often come to a library instruction session feeling like they are already expert searchers. True to their claim, they can usually Google information on any topic in less than 10 seconds. This exercise builds on a skill that the students already possess—searching the Internet—to provide a springboard for introducing library resources and evaluation criteria into their current search practices. Comparing, contrasting, and providing alternatives allows the results to speak for themselves and also allows the students to make their own choices in future searching.

COOKING TIME

Cooking time is 50 minutes and can focus on any subject. Serves fifteen to twenty-five first-year students.

ACRL INFORMATION DIETARY STANDARDS ADDRESSED

Standard Two.
Standard Three.

MAIN COOKING TECHNIQUE

Instructor demonstration, small group collaboration and student presentation

MAIN INGREDIENTS

- Presentation computer (tablet preferred) with Internet access and projector
- One computer with open Internet access for each group of students

PREPARATION

- Select a question related to the theme of the class and prepare a blank Power Point slide or Word document with the question across the top.
- To save time, prepare canned searches related to the theme in each of the resources that you will demonstrate.
- Prepare a thorough course guide, either online or in handout format, listing all the resources demonstrated in the class plus any other resources or information that the students could need.

THE INSTRUCTION SESSION

1. Begin by having the students identify key terms in the sample question and brainstorm a list of synonyms and related topics. A tablet PC is helpful for underlining, highlighting, and listing (5-10 minutes).

2. Leaving the results of the brainstorming session on the screen, form students into five groups. Without introducing any library sources or providing any instruction, ask the groups to locate different types of information related to the sample question. Encourage them to search as they normally would, whether that's starting with Google or anywhere else (5 minutes).

   a. Group 1: Find a scholarly article
   b. Group 2: Find background information
   c. Group 3: Find a book
   d. Group 4: Find an opinion
   e. Group 5: Find a Web site

3. Beginning with the first group, ask one representative to come to the presentation computer and demonstrate how the group searched, and what they found (if anything). Use the group's search technique and results as a springboard to dialogue with the class about the nature of the search and the type of information found (or not found). For example, ask the class why they think the result for the scholarly article search is actually a scholarly article or not, and why.

Briefly demonstrate a search with a selected library resource as an alternative to locating the specific type of information. If the group used a library resource in their example, demonstrate some relevant additional features (such as citation formatting) of that resource. Repeat with each of the five groups.

ALLERGY WARNINGS

It is very important to remain objective during this exercise and not to criticize students' work. Building trust with the students is essential, and an open dialogue is necessary to obtain authentic answers from the class. When viewing the results of their searches, always thank the students for their participation. Instead of responding to a search with "No, that's not a scholarly article," try leading out with "Let's see if we can find the author of this article" or something similar.

CHEF'S NOTE

- Breaking the reporting/demonstrating into five short segments provides a good change every few minutes and helps to keep the students on track. The students will often find interesting resources that stimulate evaluative discussion.

- After the class, you can keep track of noteworthy searches or issues that arose during the class time as a needs assessment. I often keep track of where the groups began their searches, what type of search they performed, and if they were able to locate a credible source before instruction.

- A variation with which I have had much success is substituting a short, relevant, current article related to the class theme in place of the initial brainstorming question. I have the class read the article and then ask them what it's about. I write down their answers verbatim, and then have them pick out which words can be used as keywords, which I circle, and which words they wouldn't include in a search, which I cross out.

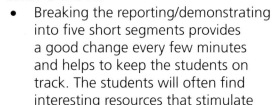

Sauté Your Own Search Interface

This recipe uses graphics to help students to think about the advanced functions of a search interface.

Shannon Pritting, Coordinator of Access Services, State University of New York College at Oswego, pritting@oswego.edu
Karen Shockey, Coordinator of Instruction, State University of New York College at Oswego, shockey@oswego.edu

NUTRITION INFORMATION

This recipe is intended to introduce students to the finer points of using database search functions to maximize and efficiently use their time spent on research to produce the best results for specific research needs. Many students, especially freshmen, resist the idea of using databases for their research needs. They have grown accustomed to using Google.

COOKING TIME

Cooking time is 60 minutes and best serves freshmen who are willing to think graphically.

ACRL INFORMATION DIETARY STANDARDS ADDRESSED

Standard One: 1.1.
Standard Two: 2.1, 2.2, 2.3.

MAIN COOKING TECHNIQUE

Mini-demonstration, small-group work, peer assistance, presentations

MAIN INGREDIENTS

- Student computers
- Microsoft Publisher or Powerpoint software (or a similar desktop publishing software could be used)
- Pre-made images of different search interface functions
- An instructor's station with projector
- Preferably some kind of screen sharing software
- If no screen sharing software is available, a flash drive to collect presentations for display for the entire class

PREPARATION

- Create images representing useful features within a search interface (e.g., date ranges, publication type, etc.). Also, review interfaces for changes and improvements so that the elements available to students for building their own search interface resembles databases the library owns.
- Create a list of specific information needs (e.g., book review on specific title from publications from different regions of the US).
- Load the images of useful features from search interfaces on the desktop of the classroom computers.
- Create directions for the project. Directions should include how to create interfaces in the software, as well as general instructions.

THE INSTRUCTION SESSION

1. Review the differences between search interfaces. Show the difference between Google, a journal database, and the catalog.
2. Review how effectively using the features of search interfaces can improve searching.
3. Introduce specific information needs and how one might use different search strategies and features most effectively to find the needed information.
4. Introduce the activity.
5. Break class into groups of three to four to make their own ideal search interface for a specific information need.
6. After groups work on creating their own ideal interfaces, bring them back together as a large group.
7. Students present and explain the interfaces they designed and how their creations would help them find the assigned specific information (book review, scholarly journal, etc.).
8. Look at some of the Library Search Interfaces to show how the functions in these interfaces are designed for specific needs.

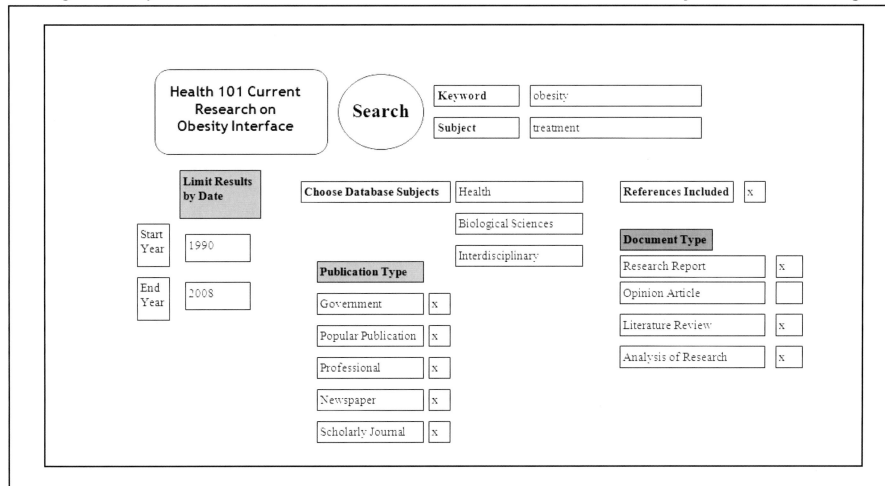

ALLERGY WARNINGS

- Students may have trouble getting started. Provide them with some examples. Remember that almost all are familiar with the Google interface.

CHEF'S NOTE

Although this recipe may seem to present a simple task, students usually leave thinking about how they should search resources differently depending on what they need to find, and will begin to look at interfaces critically. I've often found that many students end up designing interfaces that are much like the interfaces from the library databases, but can now identify how and why using advanced search features improves searching. But without this activity, only advanced searchers will look for the various limiters and functionality contained in these databases.

Whet Their Appetites: A Warm-Up Appetizer

This is an appetizer intended for students drifting into an information literacy session to do while they wait for their classmates to show up.

Jenifer Sigafoes Phelan, Education Liaison/Remote Services Librarian, Seattle Pacific University Library, sigafoes@spu.edu

NUTRITION INFORMATION
The purpose of this activity is to provide an opportunity for the students to stretch and warm up their instruction muscles as well as whet their appetites for information prior to a session.

COOKING TIME
Cooking time is 1 -15 minutes depending on how early they arrive, followed by 2-5 minutes of discussion.

ACRL INFORMATION DIETARY STANDARDS ADDRESSED
Standard One.
Standard Two.

MAIN COOKING TECHNIQUE
Hands-on practice activity, verbal sharing with the group

MAIN INGREDIENTS
- Computer access for each student with Internet access
- Worksheet for each student

PREPARATION
Choose a topic for the students to research. One sample worksheet states, "Sit at a computer and search for information about 'No Child Left Behind' then record on the chart below what you have found, where you found it, and how useful this information would be for a research paper."

THE INSTRUCTION SESSION
1. Hand each arriving student a worksheet. When it is time to start the session announce you will be taking a few minutes to go over the warm-up activity.
2. Go around the room quickly. Ask for first name, research area of interest and ask where they began their research on the pre-activity worksheet.
3. It is necessary to keep it moving along, but I find many interesting points are raised and the students usually remind each other of good online resources.
4. Alternative: To keep it short you can ask a few volunteers to share their experience and not go around the entire group.

ALLERGY WARNINGS
Once you are on the clock and your session has begun, keep the discussion moving.

CHEF'S NOTE
This is a highly recommended activity for transitional groups of students who are ready to benefit from thinking ahead to the more rigorous types of research they will need to do in the new level of education they are entering.

On the Campaign Trail: Parboiling Popular Presidential Pundits

Although Presidential elections only occur every four years, they provide relevant and researchable topics for library sessions.

Beth E. Tumbleson, Assistant Director, Gardner-Harvey Library, Miami University Middletown, Ohio, tumbleb@muohio.edu

NUTRITION INFORMATION
Often students are unfamiliar with the multiple ways of searching the online catalog, full-text databases, and electronic reference collections. Because students prefer hands-on learning but may not have an immediate and specific need to research, this exercise engages their interest and enables them to develop essential research skills.

COOKING TIME
Boiling time is 60 minutes and serves twenty-four freshmen.

ACRL INFORMATION DIETARY STANDARDS ADDRESSED
Standard One.
Standard Two.
Standard Three.

MAIN COOKING TECHNIQUE
Worksheet-based, hands-on, interactive learning which involves applying database search techniques and critical thinking

MAIN INGREDIENTS
- 1 Instructor with enthusiasm for Information Literacy
- 1 Class of freshmen willing to work outside their comfort zone
- 1 Instruction Librarian
- 1 Computer lab with twenty-four workstations
- 1 Well-thought-out worksheet
- Pinch of Curiosity
- Dash of Humor

PREPARATION
Before creating a worksheet, decide which databases are particularly appropriate. For example, if candidates have authored books, begin research in the library catalog.

THE INSTRUCTION SESSION
1. Provide a brief overview of the need to research efficiently and ethically using academic resources.
2. Indicate the numerous print and electronic resources available to students. Demonstrate how to search for various types of information.
3. Allow students to work through the worksheet. Circulate among students and provide guidance and encouragement.
4. Garnish with Reflection and Class Discussion.

ALLERGY WARNINGS
This recipe works best during a Presidential or other popular election.

CHEF'S NOTE
Begin your worksheet with a scenario: You have decided to make a difference, to exercise your responsibilities as a citizen, and vote in the upcoming presidential election. Consequently, you make the decisive move to become an informed voter and put your research skills to work. Use the Library Web site as your gateway to the information world of academic, authoritative electronic resources.

3. CITATIONS AND PLAGIARISM

Broken Citations: Recreating a Bibliography

Using parts of a bibliography as puzzle pieces, students recreate a citation and then track it down in a database.

Dr. Smita Avasthi, Reference, Instruction & Electronic Resources Librarian, Southwestern Oregon Community College, savasthi@socc.edu

NUTRITION INFORMATION

This recipe teaches students how to read and use a bibliography as a research tool with a hands-on activity. Students are asked to put together the pieces of broken citations and re-create a bibliography. They need to work together to track down the original source so they can put the pieces of the broken citation into their correct places.

COOKING TIME

Cooking time is a maximum of 60 minutes. Serves a class of fifteen to twenty-five underclassmen.

ACRL INFORMATION DIETARY STANDARDS ADDRESSED

Standard Two: 2.1, 2.2, 2.4, 2.5
Standard Five: 5.3.

MAIN COOKING TECHNIQUE

Demonstration, hands-on group activity, reflection

MAIN INGREDIENTS

- 1 sample bibliography in a specific style with entries for newspapers, articles, and books
- 1 sample bibliography in the same style with entries for resources that can be located in the school's library
- 1 hat, bag, or jar
- 1 computer classroom
- Access to a bibliographic composer or software (optional)

PREPARATION

1. Create one sample bibliography and keep it intact. Make a sufficient number of photocopies for the class session.
2. Create another bibliography with entries that can be found in the library. Separate the components of the other bibliography so that each part is on its individual line (i.e., the author's name is on a different line than the article title, which is on a different line than the journal title, etc.). Cut up the bibliography so each line is on its own scrap of paper. Fold the scraps of paper and place into the hat, bag, or jar.

THE INSTRUCTION SESSION

1. **Identify parts of a citation**. Using the intact sample bibliography, ask students to identify the kind of resource described by the entry and to explain each of the parts of the citation. For instance, ask them to differentiate between the title of an article and the title of the journal, or the retrieval date and the publication date. Show students how to find that resource at the library. Go over at least a few different kinds of entries and show students how to locate online articles in a database by using an on-

line journal locator, searching within a specific field for journal titles, searching multiple fields at once, etc.

2. **Distribute puzzle pieces**. Distribute entries from the broken bibliography by asking each student to take a scrap of paper from the hat, bag, or jar.

3. **Form working groups**. Tell students that their mission is to find the missing parts that they will need to reconstruct the original citation. To match the pieces up, they will need to work together because no one will have enough information to find the original resource on their own. They can use any method they choose to discover if they've pieced together the proper citation. Since the library owns the item on the bibliography, they should be able to locate it by using the catalog or a database. They will need to keep regrouping until they can reconstruct the citation.

4. **Reconstruct entries**. Ask students to tape the broken citation back together again on a piece of colored cardstock. Have them tape the reconstructed citations at the front of the room, making sure to order the entries alphabetically and to use a hanging indent. This way, the class can view the reconstructed bibliography at the end of the session.

5. **Group reports**. Discuss methods used by the groups to reconstruct entries and point out other options. Indicate that this exercise would have been much easier if they had had the complete citation, explaining that each component in a bibliography may be necessary to find an article, depending on what method is used and what resources the library has available.

6. **Conclusion**. Use the exercise to explain why bibliographies require detailed information. Explain that bibliographies are used as a form of scholarly communication. Discuss documentation, plagiarism, and bibliographic management software.

ALLERGY WARNINGS

Students will be quite disconcerted when they first see the minimal amount of information on the scrap of paper they picked from the jar. Be prepared to help them find their first group, particularly for a larger class. If you end up with leftover pieces after students have all picked up a scrap, participate in the activity by offering the extra part to a group that is missing a piece. The class will find it much easier to put together a citation after one has been properly pieced back together, as fewer broken bits are circulating.

CHEF'S NOTE

I like this exercise because it treats bibliographies as a research tool, which encourages students to go beyond searching by keyword. It lets them see that they can find information in multiple ways, which gives them a better sense of how information is organized. That the activity may also demonstrate the rationale behind the bibliography is an added benefit. I also favor this lesson because it encourages activity and group work. I have found that many students enjoy the active participation involved in this unexpected exercise, especially if they can see how it is relevant to furthering their research. Although they are somewhat reluctant to leave their computer screens and work together, they express a sense of accomplishment by piecing the citation back together, and the hands-on experience of searching the database in multiple fields seemed to increase their confidence.

Bibliographic Barbecue

This recipe provides students with a thorough overview of citing sources in APA style while preparing research reports.

Cassandra Jackson, Circulation/Reference Librarian, Hollis F. Price Library, LeMoyne-Owen College in Memphis, TN, cassandra_jackson@loc.edu

NUTRITION INFORMATION

Memphis is known for the Blues, Barbecue, and Beale Street. Freshman year is filled with Pizza, Parties, and Papers! For many students, the transition from high school to college in regards to preparing a research paper can be a bit challenging! Many freshmen are not familiar with the elements of a college-level research paper. They have never been introduced to various citation formats or presented with in-depth explanations on the seriousness of plagiarism. In addition, they tend not to be aware of how to properly format bibliographic citations used in their research. This recipe was developed to introduce students to the basics of the American Psychological Association citation format. Like the process of preparing great barbecue, students create accurate bibliographic citations through a precise mixture of concentration and attention to detail.

COOKING TIME

Cooking time is 60 minutes and serves fifteen students.

ACRL INFORMATION DIETARY STANDARDS ADDRESSED

Standard Two: 2:5.
Standard Five: 5:2.

MAIN COOKING TECHNIQUE

Lecture/Demonstration, small group activity

MAIN INGREDIENTS

- PowerPoint presentation (Five slides: Definition of plagiarism, Book in APA format, Electronic journal in APA format, Newspaper in APA format, Magazine in APA format)
- Teachers station
- Computer access for students (optional)
- Handouts (Bibliographic Barbecue Worksheets, Plagiarism Policy, Internet resources)
- Five American Psychological Association Manuals (one for each table)
- CD Player, Ludacris single (CD), "Stand Up"

PREPARATION

After the worksheet is finished, this workshop requires very little preparation. The worksheet lists bibliographic records in a table format. Each record represents a typical resource, such as a journal. Leave room to have each group reformat the information provided into the proper APA style.

THE INSTRUCTION SESSION

1. *Marinade*: Play Ludacris single "Stand Up" as students enter the session.

2. After all students have entered the room, ask them if they are familiar with the artist or the song. Explain to them hip-hop artist, Ludacris was sued for stealing the lyrics to the song.

3. Present the first slide—a definition of plagiarism. Have students view the handout detailing your college/university or classroom policy regarding plagiarism.

4. **Grill:** Present a mini-lecture (maximum 10 minutes). Explain to students one method of preventing plagiarism is to appropriately cite research sources. Show students examples of how to cite the following resources in APA style, highlighting the organizational format and key elements.
   - Book
   - Newspaper
   - Electronic Journal Article
   - Magazine

5. Separate students into groups and instruct them to read the instructions for the *Bibliographic Barbecue* handout. Challenge each group to refer to the lecture, APA manual, or internet resources to correctly format each citation on the worksheet.

6. The first group to correctly format each citation on the worksheet will be crowned *Bibliographic Barbecue Champs*.

7. **Simmer:** After the *Bibliographic Barbecue Champs* have been announced, the Ludacris song should be turned back on at a low volume. Inform students that Ludacris won his case. The court ruled he did not steal the lyrics to the song "Stand Up." Students should be reminded they have been given tools to prevent plagiarism and should not risk the consequences of being accused of stealing someone's work.

ALLERGY WARNINGS
The research process can cause many new researchers to be nervous. In addition, students may not be aware of the serious consequences related to plagiarism. Initially, they may not be receptive to the workshop or view it as necessary to complete their assignment.

CHEF'S NOTE
The Ludacris song is used to bring a bit of reality to the presentation. Most students are familiar with the hip-hop artist and his music. They were not able to connect the serious consequences until I explained the circumstances surrounding his single, "Stand Up."

I enjoy teaching the class because it bridges the gap between writing in high school and college. It brings to light the responsibility associated with producing college work to freshman students. Once students leave the session, they are enlightened. Many approach the reference desk with more questions related to the workshop topic.

Ludacris. "Stand Up," 2003. *Chicken-n-Beer*, Def Jam, B0000AQS1A.

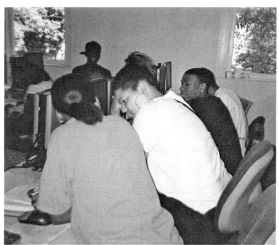

Citation Station Deluxe

Students rotate among five stations learning a different skill at each one.

Catherine Johnson, Reference/Instruction Librarian, University of Baltimore, cajohnson@ubalt.edu

NUTRITION INFORMATION

To complete this recipe with panache you need to prepare five stations in a classroom detailing five aspects of citing bibliographic resources. Students rotate between the stations until they have worked through each station's information. You have the privilege of working with students individually as they need help.

COOKING TIME

Cooking time is at least 90 minutes. Serves a class of twenty students.

ACRL INFORMATION DIETARY STANDARDS ADDRESSED

Standard Five: 5.2, 5.3.

MAIN COOKING TECHNIQUE

Small-group work, peer assistance, cooperative learning, worksheet/activity based instruction

MAIN INGREDIENTS

- Computers
- Printer access
- Citation manual (manual, online, handout, etc.)
- Five activities with written directions

PREPARATION

Set up five citation stations. Each station will have the necessary materials (including magazine articles, journal articles, book chapters etc.) and a sheet explaining the directions detailing what to do at each station, plus answer keys. Response sheets should be done in a word processing program. The stations are as follows:

1. **Citation Creation**
   Part 1—Ask students to create citations for a book, book chapter, and journal article.
   Part 2—Ask students to create citations for a magazine article, newspaper article, and website. One periodical should be a printout from a library database.

2. **References Correction**
   Students are given a references page and asked to correct all mistakes they can find. This may include formatting, title etc.

3. **In-Text Citation Insertion**
   Ask students to insert correct in-text citations into a paper. Students should be provided with a paragraph of text

taken from a fictional paper. Quotations, paraphrases, and summaries will be highlighted and will correspond in color to the original source.

4. **Understanding Citations**
   Ask students to respond to a series of questions dealing with citations. These may include, but are not limited to: "Why do we use citations?" "If you come across something you don't know how to cite, what should you do?" "Is it necessary to cite images?" "Is it necessary to cite yourself?"

5. **Plagiarism and Academic Integrity**
   Here students can gain information about academic integrity by taking a tutorial that the university has already developed. If there is not a readily available tutorial, this station can consist of a number of scenarios. Students can determine whether the people in the scenario acted with academic integrity or not.

THE INSTRUCTION SESSION

1. Review importance and purpose of citations with class. Emphasize that they need to know where to find the resources needed to create the citations. Review the citation manual of choice with the class. Explain the activity (no more than 5 minutes.)

2. Students will break up into groups.

3. Each group will begin at any of the five stations. The order in which they travel through the stations is of little importance, as long as they visit them all. Depending on the length of the class, allow students to stay at each station for 10-15 minutes before asking them to rotate.

4. Students will follow the instructions on the handouts at each station and work together to complete the task at hand.

5. As students move through each of the stations, the librarian should move through the classroom offering students guidance when needed.

6. When students have completed all five stations, they will print a copy of the work the group has completed. It is only necessary to print one copy per group.

7. The librarian will provide a copy of the correct answers to all of the questions and students will compare their responses to those from the librarian. Any discrepancies can be discussed as a group and then, if not resolved, brought to the attention of the instructor/librarian.

8. Allow about five minutes at the end of the class to discuss and reflect on the activity. Often individual students have questions that will be useful for the whole group.

ALLERGY WARNINGS

Students may feel they already know citations. Remind them that this can be used as a refresher and challenge them to take their knowledge to the next level by finding something they don't already know or help others in the group.

CHEF'S NOTE

• Many students would rather not learn about citations. However, they admit to having a much clearer idea regarding how to cite and why citations are important after attending this session.

• It has proven to be beneficial if this activity can be tied to a class grade in some way. If it's not feasible to tie the activity to a class grade, Citation Station Deluxe can be run as a contest on the class day with a small prize (candy works well!). Rather than students reviewing their own completed work, they can hand off their work to another group to review. The group with the fewest errors and the most completed answers will be named the winner.

• While there is admittedly quite a bit of prep work before using Citation Station Deluxe the first time, this work can be reused time and time again.

Bib Salad: Finding the Full Text of the Sources *They* Cited

Provide a bowl of fresh and tasty citations as a dessert to students decoding bibliographies.

Stephanie Rosenblatt, Education Librarian, California State University, Fullerton, srosenblatt@fullerton.edu

NUTRITION INFORMATION

This mini-lesson is best served as a dessert because it gives students a chance to synthesize what they've learned in the library instruction session. Students work in pairs to decode a citation from a peer-reviewed article in their subject area. They first determine the origins of the citation: journal article, monograph, chapter in a book, then they decide which library system to use to find the full-text or catalog record. The goal of this activity is to provide guided-practice so students gain experience using bibliographies to find additional sources. This exercise can be used with students at any level because the librarian can limit the type of items to be found in response to the requirements of the students' assignment or their understanding of library resources.

COOKING TIME

Cooking time is 15-20 minutes. Serves up to twice as many students as the number of computers in your lab.

ACRL INFORMATION DIETARY STANDARDS ADDRESSED

Standard Two: 2.1, 2.3, 2.5.

MAIN COOKING TECHNIQUE

Mini-lesson, work in pairs in a computer lab

MAIN INGREDIENTS

- Computer lab
- Instructor station with projector
- Citation style handout
- Slides of citation examples
- Bowl of fresh, tasty citations

PREPARATION

Prepare a handout that gives students examples of citations. Prepare a short slide show that gives examples of citations for different types of items. For the bowl of citations: print out a bibliography from a peer-reviewed journal article that relates to the subject the students are studying. Use a large font, and cut into strips (one citation per strip).

THE INSTRUCTION SESSION

1. Hand out citation style worksheet. Talk about the importance of a bibliography. Researchers use bibliographies to talk to each other across time.

2. Show an example of one type of citation on the screen (journal article, book chapter, book, etc.) and ask students to tell you what type of item is being cited.

3. Encourage them to look at their citation style sheet and elicit clues that can be used to determine the type of citation.

4. Model finding the item in your library's System (e.g., catalog for books, Find Journals by Title to determine the database your article will be found in, etc.).

5. Repeat until all citation types needed for this particular class/assignment have been covered.

6. Break students into pairs. Hand each pair either one or two citations from the bowl, depending on the time available. Tell the students they now have to find the full-text or catalog record of the item. Make it a race, if they need extra motivation.

7. Walk around to see how students are doing and nudge them toward the right tool if necessary. Students can tell when they've been successful.

ALLERGY WARNINGS

It's a good idea to make sure that your library provides access to the materials included in the bowl of citations, unless you're open to a teachable moment and have time to launch into an explanation of interlibrary loan or WorldCat.

CHEF'S NOTE

- I've used this activity with upper and lower division undergraduates and graduate students. I like it because it gives students an opportunity to decide which of the many tools they have begun using during the library instruction session are appropriate for solving their problem, while providing structured practice of a skill that many of them will use—being able to decipher another researcher's bibliography.

- I think that letting the students work in pairs allows them to feel more comfortable exploring the library's Web site and making mistakes. It's also easy for me to informally assess the students and correct any misunderstandings while I'm walking around the room.

- Most people like playing games, and I'm willing to try anything that can add a little fun to even a late night instruction session. It makes it more interesting for me if I choose citations from an article that relates to the topics the students are researching. I've had some students hoard their citations so they could find the items again and use them in their papers.

Sugar and Spice and How to Cite Nice

This recipe actually consists of two activities which blend to make a fine meal. The first course teaches students about paraphrasing resources. The second course compares a citation to a puzzle.

Elaine Kushmaul, Central Piedmont Community College, Elaine.kushmaul@cpcc.edu
Steven Osler, Central Piedmont Community College, Steve.osler@cpcc.edu

NUTRITION INFORMATION

This instruction recipe offers hands-on experience with identifying proper paraphrasing and creating a citation in the correct format. The session is intended for classes who have already been introduced to using library resources and who are ready to begin working on a research paper.

COOKING TIME

Cooking time is 60 minutes and serves no more than twenty-five students.

ACRL INFORMATION DIETARY STANDARDS ADDRESSED

Standard Five: 5.2, 5.3.

MAIN COOKING TECHNIQUE

Lecturette, small-group work, presentations

MAIN INGREDIENTS

- Paraphrase or Plagiarism? Worksheets & Highlighters
- Guides for Creating Citations (Use your preferred guide)
- Citation Puzzle Pieces
- Flip Chart Paper and Markers

PREPARATION

1. Prepare introductory remarks about the importance of using citations (see next section).
2. Gather supplies.
   a. For each *team*
      i. 1 Set of Citation Puzzle Pieces
      ii. 1 "Paraphrase or Plagiarism" worksheet
      iii. 1 Highlighter
      iv. 1 Flipchart and Marker
   e. For each *student*
      i. 1 Citation guide of your choosing (handout, webpage, etc...)

THE INSTRUCTION SESSION

1. **Activity 1**
   a. Introductory Remarks
      i. Review the purpose of citations
         A. Explain how citations are like breadcrumbs: parenthetical leads to works cited, which leads to the source. (We visually display this, using actual examples.)
      ii. Review how to properly paraphrase
         A. For example, put the author's ideas in your own words, changing one or two words is not paraphrasing. Paraphrased material still needs a citation, etc.
      iii. Review when to use citations
         A. For example, after paraphrased material, directly after quotes, etc.
   a. Group Activity 1 — Paraphrase or Plagiarism? Worksheet
      i. Students collaborate to identify which passage is plagiarized and which is properly paraphrased.
      ii. Each group presents their conclusions to the class.

2. Activity 2

a. Introductory remarks

   i. Instructor illustrates proper format for a citation in a works cited page.

b. Group Activity 2

   i. Instructor gives students a guide on how to cite sources in a particular format. This could be a website, handout or even the MLA or APA manual.

   ii. Each group is given a sample source (article, book, Web page, etc.) and one set of citation puzzle cards.

   iii. Using their citation guide, each group correctly arranges the puzzle cards to make a citation for their sample source. Each puzzle card has one part of a citation written on it (author, title, access date, etc.). The students may have more cards than are needed for their particular source. For example, a magazine will not need the "publisher" puzzle card. Once each group has the pieces arranged, they can write the corresponding information on the cards in the proper format.

   iv. Groups will then write the complete citation for their example source on flip chart paper and present to class.

ALLERGY WARNINGS

Works best as a Just-In-Time class when students are currently working on an assignment requiring a bibliography.

CHEF'S NOTE

- The "Paraphrase or Plagiarism? Worksheet" engages the students and creates observable "Aha" moments.

- Going through the steps to create a citation in a group and presenting it to the class, builds students' confidence that they can properly give credit for resources used.

- Leaving the students with citation guides for later reference is also important since it is impossible to cover every variation in the class.

- It helps put the students at ease to remind them that they don't need to memorize all the rules for each citation type, it's more important to know how to find the rules and follow the process when needed.

Paraphrase or Plagiarism? Worksheet Sample

Original Passage	1.)	2.)
When taking notes only copy word for word from a source if you plan on using the material as a quote in your assignment. -Fran Miller	Exact transcribing of source material within your notes is only recommended if you are considering quoting the author.	Exact transcribing of source material within your notes is only recommended if you are considering quoting the author (Miller 87).

Plagiarism Happens: Don't Let it Happen to You

It's easy to find instances of plagiarism on YouTube. Since most students can easily navigate the Web, this is a good place to start the discussion.

Elaine Kushmaul, Central Piedmont Community College, Elaine.kushmaul@cpcc.edu
Steven Osler, Central Piedmont Community College, Steve.osler@cpcc.edu

NUTRITION INFORMATION

This instruction recipe provides students with an opportunity to understand plagiarism through discovery and discussion of real-world examples.

COOKING TIME

Cooking time is at least 60 minutes and serves no more than twenty-five students.

ACRL INFORMATION DIETARY STANDARDS ADDRESSED

Standard Five: 5.2, 5.3.

MAIN COOKING TECHNIQUE

Mini-demonstration, small-group work, presentations

MAIN INGREDIENTS

- Computer with Internet connectivity and audio for each team
- Instructor's station w/ video projector and speakers

PREPARATION

- Prepare suggestions for search terms: such as, "music and plagiarism," "politics and plagiarism," etc.
- Also, have ready some multimedia examples of plagiarism to get participants started searching.

THE INSTRUCTION SESSION

1. **Introductory remarks**
   a. Define plagiarism with a multimedia example from YouTube.
   b. Discuss the types of plagiarism (Intentional, Unintentional, Cyber, Self).
   c. Address the consequences of plagiarism at your institution and in society.

2. **Group Activity**
   a. Rules for activity—Each team will use YouTube to find an example of plagiarism in popular culture (music, movies, political speeches, etc.) then use the open Internet to find some background information about the circumstances surrounding the situation.
   b. A spokesperson from each group will use the instructor's station to show the example to the rest of the class, discuss the type of plagiarism, circumstances, consequences, and how the situation could have been avoided.

ALLERGY WARNINGS

You must be aware of time constraints to allow all groups to present. YouTube content may be objectionable to some students; tell each group to "Keep it clean."

CHEF'S NOTE

The first time the recipe was used, it was followed by another class session for the same instructor, using a lecture style to teach the topic of plagiarism. Feedback from the faculty member indicated that the more active session generated increased engagement and discussion from the students as compared to the other class.

We found that some teams of students had trouble finding examples on their own, so in the future we will have multiple suggestions ready to share.

4. EVALUATING VARIOUS TYPES OF RESOURCES

Wikipedia v. Google v. The Library: Who's your Research SuperChef?

This appetizer has students judging Wikipedia, Google, and the Library as the "Top Place on the Web to Do Research." Groups brainstorm and then present their findings to the class.

Carrie Donovan, Instructional Services Librarian, Indiana University Bloomington, cdonovan@indiana.edu
Rachel M. Slough, Graduate Asst., Reference and Instructional Services, Indiana University Bloomington, rslough@indiana.edu

NUTRITION INFORMATION

This recipe will assist students to learn how Wikipedia and Google can be used as effective starting points for a basic search, and to realize that many of the search skills they already have apply to library research.

COOKING TIME

Cooking time is 30 minutes, if demonstrations are included. Serves as many as sixty undergraduate students.

ACRL INFORMATION DIETARY STANDARDS ADDRESSED

Standard One: 1.1, 1.2.

MAIN COOKING TECHNIQUE

Small and large group discussion, possibly some demonstration
Standard Two: 2.1.

MAIN INGREDIENTS

- Whiteboard/Blackboard
- Prizes. Marketing giveaways are helpful here, but instructional handouts (Limited edition! Autographed by a librarian!) usually get laughs from the students

PREPARATION

Divide the board into columns, one each for Wikipedia, Google, and the Library. This can also be done while students discuss.

THE INSTRUCTION SESSION

1. Ask the students where they usually find information. If they don't immediately answer "Google, Wikipedia or the Library," gently guide them in that direction.
2. Divide the class into three groups.
3. Explain that each group represents one of the above-mentioned places to find information. The challenge is to argue why their assigned source is the "Top Place on the Web to Do Research." Why their assigned source is the SuperChef of research. They have 5-10 minutes to do this.
4. Emphasize that this is a competition and points (and/or prizes) will be awarded.
5. Bring the class together. Have each team in turn present their ideas, awarding a tally mark in the appropriate column (i.e. Library, Google, Wikipedia) for each idea presented.
6. If needed, add more ideas for the library to ensure it has the most tally marks and/or to balance out other sources.
7. Count the final number of tally marks in each column to determine a winner. If using prizes, distribute to all students.

ALLERGY WARNINGS

Students, especially students in early morning classes, may be reluctant to participate. Be prepared to jump in and prompt.

CHEFS' NOTE

Most students seem to embrace the competitive spirit of this recipe and the chance to validate Wikipedia and Google. We have gotten cheers and applause from some particularly enthusiastic classes. This activity can be quite flexible, easily adapted to a variety of time limits and topics. It also gives the chance to present a more approachable face to students if you cheer on groups, joke with the students, and provide encouragement throughout the process. It may serve as a way of gauging how much the students already know about the library.

Google vs. Academic Search Premier: The Evaluation Challenge

Student groups search for resources with Google and with Academic Search Premier. They then compare the credibility of the results.

Andrea Falcone, Virtual Services Librarian, Western Illinois University, Macomb, IL, A-Falcone@wiu.edu

NUTRITION INFORMATION
This recipe promotes the evaluation of electronic resources, provides students with an opportunity to think critically about information gathering tools, and gives them experience articulating the differences between resources.

COOKING TIME
Cooking time is 50 minutes and serves up to thirty students.

ACRL INFORMATION DIETARY STANDARDS ADDRESSED
Standard One.
Standard Two.
Standard Three.
Standard Four.

MAIN COOKING TECHNIQUE
Group work, class discussion, presentations

MAIN INGREDIENTS
- Computer access for all students
- Instructor workstation
- Blackboard/Whiteboard

PREPARATION
You will need to have topics (at least four) and handouts ready in advance.

THE INSTRUCTION SESSION
1. As students arrive, have them sit in groups and start brainstorming about different types of resources (Web pages, journal articles, newspaper articles, book reviews, etc.) that can be found on the Web or in a library database, such as Academic Search Premier.
2. Have students name the resources and write them on the board. Use this opportunity to briefly discuss characteristics of these resources and how to evaluate the resources based on these characteristics. Students will be able to refer to these notes during the rest of the session (10 minutes.)
3. Hand out topics and worksheets for recording results.
4. Students should discuss the assigned topic and come up with keywords for conducting their searches. This is a good opportunity to help them focus on the important concepts (3-5 minutes.)
5. Students are to search Google and Academic Search Premier and record four of the most relevant results from each search. Then they are to evaluate the credibility of each result. Students may need to be shown how to access

Academic Search Premier from the library's web site (15 minutes.)
6. Students will need to decide which search tool was easier and produced the most credible results (3 minutes.)
7. Students will present their results to the class. Keep a tally of how many times groups choose Google or Academic Search Premier as their favorite tool (15-20 minutes.)

ALLERGY WARNINGS
The topics need to be presented within some context, so that students can isolate the key concepts and come up with various search terms. It is important that the groups are ready to present their results, so watching the time and keeping students on track is necessary.

CHEF'S NOTE
Students are generally surprised that they get more results that are relevant after spending a short amount of time brainstorming to come up with various search terms. They are also surprised that evaluating results from Academic Search Premier is much easier and faster than evaluating results from the Web.

To Google or Not to Google: That is the Question! (A Wiki Can Help You Decide)

One student commented, "I like to use [the] wiki and I know that help is always available to me. It was great to know I could go back to the tip sheets and examples if I needed. Having an online place for our group to store our results made preparing our presentation much easier."

Carolyn Meier, Instructional Services Librarian, Virginia Tech, Blacksburg, VA, cmeier@vt.edu

NUTRITION INFORMATION

Students in the Freshmen Transitions class are asked to create a presentation plus a bibliography about a typical freshmen problem. The topics range from the general (time management) to the specifically Virginia Tech issues (the dreaded Math Emporium.) This is usually the freshman's first brush with research. Their first instinct is to search Google. This is a great chance for a comparison of Google with academic databases.

COOKING TIME

Cooking time is 60 minutes and serves twenty-five students.

ACRL INFORMATION DIETARY STANDARDS ADDRESSED

Standard One: 1.0, 1.1
Standard Two: 2.0, 2.2
Standard Three: 3.0

MAIN COOKING TECHNIQUE

Wiki, mini-demonstration, small group work, hands on

MAIN INGREDIENTS

- Computer access for all students
- Instructor station with projector
- Whiteboard/chalkboard with markers/chalk
- Link to the Wiki

PREPARATION

Librarian needs to create the wiki and create student login and passwords. The wiki will include concept table examples, database tip sheets, group pages, and sample worksheets and instructions.

THE INSTRUCTION SESSION

- **Introduction:** As students enter the classroom they will be asked to sit in their assigned groups. The wiki will be open on the student computers and students will be encouraged to look through the wiki to familiarize themselves with the tasks at hand.
- Librarian will give a short introduction about creating the concept table. This is a brainstorming tool used at Virginia Tech to help students narrow topics and create

effective search strategies. Time is now given for groups to create their concept table. The librarian and student aide will circulate and be available for help.

- The librarian will then ask students where they usually go for information and why. The usual answer is Google because it is quick, comprehensive, and easy. The librarian will then give a quick demonstration of searching Academic Search Complete or Factiva, depending on the student topics. At this point of the lesson the librarian informs the students that their task will be to compare Google and an academic database for usefulness—10 minutes.
- **Group Work:** Students will have two tasks to complete during this section. Results will be posted on the group wiki pages. The librarian and student aide will circulate to answer questions and offer help—30-45 minutes.

– *Task #1*—Each group will choose one search inquiry and search a database and Google. They will evaluate the first five results from each for relativity, currency, authority, and bias. Students will also discuss the number of findings and the number they could actually use. They will make recommendations as to which returned better results—Google or the database.

– *Task #2*—Students will begin to compile their research articles. They will enter bibliographic information along with a hyperlink or URL to the article or website. They will also add a short summary (several sentences) as to why this would be a good source for their presentations.

• **Wrap-up**—Each group will present their results—advantages and disadvantages of the database and Google and which they preferred—10 minutes.

ALLERGY WARNINGS

• We were prepared for the possibility of the students' lack of familiarity with editing wikis. On the whole students did very well.

• Decide before the class how students will access the wiki. Will this wiki be open to the public or only to the class? Ours was open only to the class and the instructors.

• Rather than inviting students to the wiki, we chose to create class logins and passwords.

CHEF'S NOTE

This lesson was specifically designed to maximize the amount of time students spent interacting with the resources and limiting the amount of Librarian Speak. I really enjoyed this lesson—I like taking more of a consultant role. The students were very engaged. It was an eye opener to watch students search databases with a minimal amount of librarian assistance plus the aid of tip sheets. Less talking and lecturing allowed students to spend more time actually researching. I have now resolved to do the absolute minimum lecturing in all classes.

The student aide and I found ourselves giving more help on search strategies than database mechanics. The Google- database comparison charts were surprisingly successful. The charts allowed students to quickly see the advantages of academic databases. Most students stated that they hadn't used academic databases previously. Google was still going to be their search engine of choice for their personal needs. But for their academic needs, this group of students was going to use academic databases.

The citation page proved to be less than effective. Students were more inclined to use the e-mail functions of the databases than copying the citation into the wiki. Truthfully—e-mailing the article to their e-mail account was a much better use of their time. In later iterations of this lesson, we left the citation page out of the wiki.

Creating class wikis are worthwhile but time consuming. I assumed I would be able to duplicate the entire wiki site but was not able to do so with the chosen wiki software. I am assuming there is a way around this and I will eventually stumble onto it!

The advantage of using the class wikis is the ability to tailor the resources to the specific class assignment. These wikis were available throughout the entire semester and students were able to refer to the tip sheets as needed.

To see the wiki for this recipe, go to http://vtwing2.pbworks.com/ or contact the author.

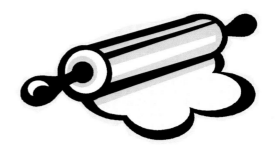

Wikipedia: Appetizer of Choice!

This recipe works best as an appetizer to start the information meal.

Sara R. Seely, Reference and Instruction Librarian, Boise State University, saraseely@boisestate.edu

NUTRITION INFORMATION

The recipe will provide students with an opportunity to get acquainted with a research topic; explore, evaluate and contribute to Wikipedia as an information resource; practice paraphrasing and citing sources in a real-world setting; and create a research strategy. Faculty who wish their students would get beyond Wikipedia will eat this up! For use in entry-level classes that covers hot topics in the news.

COOKING TIME

Cooking time is 50 to 75 minutes and serves no more than thirty students.

ACRL INFORMATION DIETARY STANDARDS ADDRESSED

Standard Three: 3.1, 3.2
Standard Four: 4.1, 4.3
Standard Five: 5.1, 5.2, 5.3

MAIN COOKING TECHNIQUE

Small group collaborative exercise, individual exercises, group discussion

MAIN INGREDIENTS

- Computer with Web access for each student
- Instructor's workstation with projector
- Post-it flipcharts or enough white board space, one for each group
- CQ Researcher (or comparable resource)
- Tables grouped for four to five people (ideal but not required)

PREPARATION

Students should have a topic in mind before the workshop. Check CQ Researcher to see if students' topics are adequately covered. If not, brainstorm alternatives, such as an interdisciplinary article database. You will also need to prepare flipcharts (or white-board space) with a large Venn diagram on each, one for each student group. Have Wikipedia open in a web browser on each computer.

THE INSTRUCTION SESSION

1. Have students sit in groups of four to five (if possible, arrange tables to accommodate).

2. As students trickle in, welcome them and ask them to find and read a Wikipedia article on their topic (5 min.)

3. As a class, open a second browser window and navigate to CQ Researcher. Find a relevant article (5 min.)

4. Working in groups, have students complete the Venn diagram on the Post-it flipchart, listing what's useful about each resource: 1) Wikipedia on one side 2) CQ Researcher on the other and 3) shared qualities in the middle (5 minutes.)

5. Each group displays their findings and Librarian leads a group discussion (10-15 minutes.) To deepen the conversation, pose questions such as these: "What would you use Wikipedia for and why? What would you use CQ Researcher for and why?"

6. Librarian demonstrates how to edit Wikipedia to include information from a CQ Researcher article and cite CQ Researcher. Or, mix it up! If a student already knows how, have the student demonstrate (5 min.)

7. Students now work individually to 1) read/skim both the CQ Researcher article and the Wikipedia article, 2) paraphrase information found in CQ Researcher and 3) edit Wikipedia to include the paraphrase and a citation for CQ Researcher (10-20 min.)

8. Wrap up! Brainstorm next steps as a class (other web resources, books, articles, etc.) Have students write down the name of a database and/or the ideal title for a book so there is a concrete next place to go for information. This piece is their Exit Ticket. Librarian stands at the door and each student reports about a resource as they leave. (10-15)

ALLERGY WARNINGS

It's easy for students to fall into the trap of telling the Librarian what they think she wants to hear—"Wikipedia is bad. Library resource is good." I try to make clear that I'm not devaluing Wikipedia but instead I'm asking students to fully articulate its value: How is it useful in my context?

CHEF'S NOTE

A high-quality group discussion is key to the success of this workshop. That said, I usually find students enjoy talking about Wikipedia because it's a source they are familiar with. Once conversation is flowing about the useful aspects of Wikipedia (e.g., topic overview, links to additional resources, 24/7 access), my challenge is then to push their thinking a bit when asking questions about the use of Wikipedia in an academic context. I've been surprised to find that while most students know that anyone can edit Wikipedia, they don't realize anyone includes them! I inevitably hear "Oh, that's easy!" from the class when I click on the Edit tab. By asking students to begin contributing to Wikipedia as a shared resource, it helps them to define the audience for the Web site and set Wikipedia in the context of other types of information found in more traditional publishing models (books, websites, etc.). An added bonus is that Wikipedia articles require authors to cite their sources, adding street cred to what sometimes seems like an ancient practice.

I Once Touched an Elephant's Trunk: Where Do Primary Sources End and Secondary Sources Begin?

This recipe makes use of several activities that help students distinguish the distance between an author and the events or subjects of which they write.

Bonnie Imler, Information Technology Librarian, Penn State Altoona, bbi1@psu.edu

NUTRITION INFORMATION

This is intended as an introduction to primary and secondary sources and is especially beneficial to undergraduates (such as, students in a History course) who are required to use primary sources for a research paper. The Telephone Game makes a quick appetizer, for the actual examination of some primary sources.

COOKING TIME

Cooking time is 60 minutes and serves no more than twenty-five students.

ACRL INFORMATION DIETARY STANDARDS ADDRESSED

Standard One: 1.2.
Standard Two: 2.1, 2.3.
Standard Three: 3.2, 3.4.

MAIN COOKING TECHNIQUE

Mini-demonstration, small-group work

MAIN INGREDIENTS

- Teaching station
- Examples of primary and secondary sources (One for every two students)

PREPARATION

Gather examples of primary and secondary sources

THE INSTRUCTION SESSION

1. **The Telephone Game**
   a. Begin session by having students lineup side-by-side.
   b. Ask students if they remember playing the Telephone Game when they were in elementary school.
   c. Briefly explain that you will be whispering a message to the first student and they need to whisper the message to the person next to them, passing it on down the line.
   d. Have the last person in line repeat the message back to you.
   e. Ask students if they were to write about the Telephone Message, who would be a primary source and who would not.

2. **Discussion**
   a. Explain that the topic for the day is primary vs. secondary sources. Give a brief explanation.
   b. Mention historic primary sources and review the difference between journals, magazines, and newspapers.

3. **Paper Primary Sources**
   a. Have students pair-up.
   b. Pass out primary and secondary examples.

c. Give a few minutes for students to analyze content.

d. Have each group report on whether their source is primary or secondary and why.

e. Collect examples.

f. Explain how students can find primary sources.

4. **Primary Sources in Other Media**

a. Mention a recent event that received a lot of media attention. (e.g., Virginia Tech tragedy)

b. Ask how each student found out about the event.

c. Ask how word of the event got to the media (phone messages, text messages, IM's, blogs, university web postings, mass e-mails, etc.).

d. Ask how these *new* primary sources can be archived.

e. Show archival web sites for the event.

f. Introduce media transcripts and show databases that will help students to find TV and news transcripts, news images, etc.

ALLERGY WARNINGS

- If students balk at the Telephone Game, pull three or four Good Sports to demonstrate.
- I find that having two students looking at one source sample works better than one or a larger group. With larger groups, only one or two students actually participate and it is embarrassing for only one student if they have selected primary or secondary incorrectly.

CHEF'S NOTE

- The activity at the start of class tends to wake-up the students and keeps them motivated.
- A long "telephone" message plus increased number of students equals a greater chance of distorted message.
- The message "I once touched an elephant's trunk" came back in one class as "I once sat in the kitchen sink" and most recently as "I watched Dr. Sullivan get drunk!"

- Most students guess that if the instructor and first student in line wrote about the original conversation that they would be considered primary sources, but do not immediately connect that the second student in line's account could also be considered primary since that student heard it from someone at the actual event. I compare this to newspaper accounts being considered primary sources. It tends to be an "Aha" moment.

- When picking primary and secondary sources as examples, include a variety of sources (diaries, works of art, case studies, autobiographies, battle logs, census records, etc.).

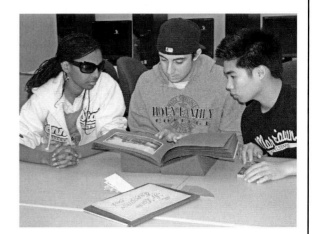

Meet the Presidents: An Introduction to Primary and Secondary Sources

"What's in those boxes?" students ask as they gather in the classroom.

Amanda Nash, Instruction Librarian, Catawba College, Salisbury, NC, manash@catawba.edu

NUTRITION INFORMATION

This recipe will introduce students to the lives of several presidents. Boxes of biographical source materials await. Each group must determine which resources are primary and which are secondary and report their findings.

COOKING TIME

Cooking time is 30 to 60 minutes and serves at least eight students and no more than thirty.

ACRL INFORMATION DIETARY STANDARDS ADDRESSED

Standard One: 1.2
Standard Three: 3.1, 3.2, 3.6
Standard Four: 4.1, 4.3

MAIN COOKING TECHNIQUE

Small group work, presentations

MAIN INGREDIENTS

- A selection of primary and secondary sources relating to U.S. presidents. The number of presidents you use for the exercise and the number of sources you select for each president will depend upon your class/group size. I like to use groups of three to five students and four to six sources per president.
- Lidded, unmarked boxes to hold the materials for each president (Highsmith has some brightly colored boxes that work nicely, or you can use banker's boxes, etc.).
- For a gourmet version, an instructor's workstation with projector and document camera could be used to enhance the group presentations.

PREPARATION

Select presidents. Pull primary and secondary sources for each president from your collection and place the materials in boxes. You need to be familiar with the sources you select so that you can work effectively with the groups as they evaluate their materials and present their findings.

THE INSTRUCTION SESSION

1. **Introduction**
   a. Discuss the definitions of primary and secondary sources, suggesting examples of each type of source. Discuss why both types of sources are important for research. Field any student questions.

2. **Activity**
   a. Divide class into groups.
   b. Have each group choose a box without opening it. The boxes are lidded and unmarked, so the contents are a surprise. At this point, students will be somewhat perplexed as to what all of this is about.
   c. Inform the students that the goal of this exercise is to Meet the Presidents. Each group will (hypothetically) explore the life and times of a particular president using both primary and secondary sources.
   d. Each box contains a selection of materials that could be used for their research. The students must determine which materials could serve as primary sources and which could serve as secondary sources.

e. The students decide how to approach and divide the workload, but the entire group must reach a consensus for each source in the box.

f. Float between the groups to answer questions and keep discussions on track.

3. **Discussion**

a. Regroup for presentations and discussion.

b. Have each group identify their president, show their materials, and explain the decisions they made about the sources in their box.

c. Prompt the groups during their presentations to elicit their reasons for labeling a source as primary or secondary.

d. Allow classmates to ask questions or dispute findings to get the entire class involved.

4. **Review**

a. Save time at the end of the activity to review what the students have learned and answer any remaining questions.

ALLERGY WARNINGS

Some students balk at working in groups, so you may have a little resistance to the activity at first, but the process of selecting the boxes usually generates some curiosity and enthusiasm. You have to interact with the groups as they are working to ensure that everyone is taking part in looking at and evaluating the sources and not just rushing to finish by allowing the more vocal students make all the decisions.

CHEF'S NOTE

When I first began teaching primary vs. secondary sources to our adult learners, I used a variety of topics for this exercise—some historical, some literary, some popular culture. I found that a number of my students were completely unfamiliar with some of the subjects I had chosen, which made them less interested and hampered their ability to evaluate the materials. I revised the activity using materials related to the presidents because all of my students at least had heard of the different presidents and often knew a bit about them, and even a small library like ours has a decent selection of materials that I could use. This exercise has worked very well for my classes so far—students who have never encountered these concepts before leave with the ability to differentiate between primary and secondary sources. And after they get involved with the materials and start to discuss their president with their peers, the students are interested and engaged.

Sardines or Salmon? What's the Difference?

This piscine recipe helps students to quickly fish out the Sardinian qualities of the Magazine and the Salmonly qualities of the Journal. Racing to the finish, students vie to display their catch on the whiteboard.

Jason Dupree, Head of Public Services and Assistant Professor, Southwestern Oklahoma State University, Weatherford, OK, jason.dupree@swosu.edu

NUTRITION INFORMATION

Composition students are asked to select a topic for a three to five page research paper assignment. This exercise takes place as students examine article databases. To assist students in understanding the fundamental differences between popular and scholarly literature, students are asked to compare a magazine and a journal to formulate an assessment on the target audience, purpose and readability of each.

COOKING TIME

Cooking time is 50 to 75 minutes and serves freshman and sophomore classes of thirty students.

ACRL INFORMATION DIETARY STANDARDS ADDRESSED

Standard One: 1.2.
Standard Three: 3.2, 3.4, 3.5, 3.6.
Standard Four: 4.2, 4.3.

MAIN COOKING TECHNIQUE

Small-group work, peer assistance

MAIN INGREDIENTS

- Dry-Erase Board/Markers.
- Multiple unbound copies of a magazine (e.g., *Wired*).
- Multiple unbound copies of a peer-reviewed journal with continuous pagination (e.g., *Journal of Orthopaedic and Sports Physical Therapy*).

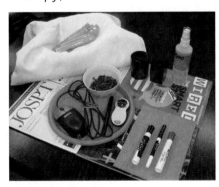

PREPARATION

Pull enough unbound copies of a magazine and a peer-reviewed journal for every student to use. Divide the dry-erase board into two areas. The title of the magazine placed at the top on the left side and the title of the journal at the top on the right side.

THE INSTRUCTION SESSION

1. **Introduction**
   a. Do a mini-lecture on the highlights of popular vs. scholarly literature—5-7 minutes.

2. **Activity**
   a. Rules
      i. Divide the class into groups of two
      ii. Upon identifying a difference, someone from the group writes the comparison on both sides of the dry-erase board (i.e., *Wired*—is a magazine; *Journal of Orthopaedic and Sports Physical Therapy*—is a journal)
      iii. Easiest answers will be taken quickly (this statement usually inspires competition between groups)
      iv. While waiting to record your findings, if another team writes your answer your team must identify something else

v. Present this exercise as a race (in our experience, some students will try to make a dash for the board before they are instructed to begin). Hold markers for the students and let them begin

b. Part 1—Examination
   i. Each group examines both publications for differences in appearance and content

c. Part 2—Identification
   i. Each group must provide a unique comparison; groups cannot duplicate answers of other teams
   ii. Groups record their findings on a whiteboard

3. **Discussion**
   a. Clarify any misunderstanding and/ or answer any questions
   b. When all groups have recorded their findings, the librarian has the right to ask questions of the class or ask the individual groups to elaborate on their choices
   c. A mini-lecture will follow with a formal presentation of all possible differences
   d. The presentation material will be matched to their findings
   e. The concluding dialogue will open to a discussion of the peer-review process.

ALLERGY WARNINGS
Students will have difficulty finding comparisons. They will need to be encouraged to think outside the box and pay attention to details. When racing to the dry-erase board, encourage the students to be mindful of their safety and that of others.

CHEF'S NOTE
Although students tend to be kinesthetic learners, they are generally unenthusiastic about doing a participatory exercise, but teaching faculty find the experience rewarding due to the students' proximity to the resources they will be using. Feedback from students indicates actual enjoyment of this activity as compared to lecture and worksheet activities. During the four part series, we realize a large amount of information is presented to students; therefore, this activity provides a break for students to use the information rather than absorb it. Students have expressed great pleasure in writing on the dry-erase board (even though it is located in front of the classroom). This exercise lends itself to random conversations, dialogues of humor, and the occasional stampede.

Grilled, Choice-Cut Periodical Strips (with Evaluation Sauce)

Students will love the smell of grilled periodicals! Students find an article. Their article is then evaluated in several ways for scholarly credibility—by a group member and then by the whole group. The group presents their most scholarly article to the whole class.

Oliver Zeff, Reference and Instruction Librarian, Westfield State College, ozeff@wsc.ma.edu

NUTRITION INFORMATION
This recipe is intended for students in a freshman composition class, who are assigned a research project which requires the use of scholarly sources. The exercise could conceivably be used in any class where a general topic database is demonstrated and scholarly sources are required.

COOKING TIME
Cooking time is 75 minutes and serves fifteen to twenty students.

ACRL INFORMATION DIETARY STANDARDS ADDRESSED
Standard Two: 2.2, 2.5.
Standard Three: 3.2, 3.6, 3.7.

MAIN COOKING TECHNIQUE
Brief demonstration, group activity, presentations

MAIN INGREDIENTS
- Five sets of cards numbered 1 through 4 (Each set a different color. Used to sort students into groups.)
- Five table tents, each describing a different evaluation criterion. Accuracy, Authority, Language, Objectivity, Relevance (Each tent's color matches a set of cards.)
- Citation Worksheets for all students
- Five sets of Evaluation Worksheets (Print enough of each for one small group)
- Accuracy Evaluation Worksheets
- Authority Evaluation Worksheets
- Language Evaluation Worksheets
- Objectivity Evaluation Worksheet
- Relevancy Evaluation Worksheets
- An electronic classroom with workstations for each student and the librarian, optimally including tables for grouping.

PREPARATION
Create number cards, table tents, and handouts. Interfile colored cards to ensure that five groups are formed.

THE INSTRUCTION SESSION
1. **Demonstrate database**—10 minutes.
   Students receive a colored number card as they enter the lab. The librarian introduces the students to a general topic database such as Academic Search Premier, discussing basic searching.
2. **Find article**—15 minutes.
   Students find an article, print it, and make note of the article's citation on a Citation Worksheet.
3. **Students evaluate articles**
   a. Students form five evaluation groups. Students take their printed article, the Citation Worksheet, and sit at the table with the same color table tent as the card they received.
      i. Accuracy Table
      ii. Authority Table
      iii. Language Table
      iv. Objectivity Table
      v. Relevancy Table
   b. Students exchange articles. Students hand their article to the person on their right.

c. **Students rate articles individually.**—3 minutes
The librarian then hands out the respective sets of Evaluation Worksheets to each table. Students are instructed to rate the article which they have just received on the two scales listed on the Evaluation Worksheet for their table criterion.

d. **Students rate articles as a group**—5 minutes
Students work as groups to complete the last section of the Worksheet according to their table criterion, e.g., "Language Table—Working with your group members, decide which of the articles you have is written for a scholarly or professional audience."

4. **Groups report to the class.**
As students report, the librarian may interview each group as necessary to help clarify or correct their decision and explanation.
   a. Criterion for their table (Read aloud the last section of the Evaluation Worksheet)
   b. Article chosen (Title and Periodical)
   c. Why the group chose this article over the others at the table

5. **Hand out a list of all the criteria,** urging students to practice this type of evaluation in their scholarly research.

ALLERGY WARNINGS

The librarian's role in the groups' reporting can be crucial. Often a group will make a poor choice as to the most scholarly article. In some cases, there will be no scholarly articles from which the group may choose. The librarian can facilitate the discussion, questioning the students' choices, asking follow-up questions, relating the groups' criteria to one another, and stressing points made by the students.

Photo by Sarah Scott

CHEF'S NOTE

- If an article is twenty pages or more, students are advised to print only the first and last two pages.
- Since this lesson's implementation, the library has received praise from faculty members who have previously experienced difficulty in directing students to the best sources of information. Informal assessment has shown an improvement in the quality of sources cited in the papers. Reference and Instruction Librarians have noticed a marked decrease in students choosing the first database results they see and an increase in students' willingness to track down a higher quality source even if the library does not own the publication.
- The exercise itself heightens student interest in the evaluation process since the articles evaluated are from their own research. Having the students switch articles with other students at the table creates a contentious dynamic that can lead to a livelier group discussion.
- The exercise can be altered to incorporate the evaluation of websites by simply allowing students to search and print out Web pages on their topic using Google.
- Corinne Ebbs contributed to the development of this recipe.

Snap or Clap: Scholarly or Popular?

This dessert recipe will test students' knowledge of the differences between Scholarly Journals and Popular Magazines. PowerPoint is used to present images that students need to identify as Journal or Magazine.

Lorin Fisher, Information Literacy Coordinator, Texas State University-San Marcos, indrani@txstate.edu

NUTRITION INFORMATION
Freshman Composition students are asked to write a paper on a topic of their choice. They must use three sources: Scholarly Journals, a Popular Magazine, and an internet source. This is also good for Intensive English (English as a Second Language) students, who have a composition assignment.

COOKING TIME
Cooking time is 15 to 20 minutes and serves less than thirty freshmen or ESL students.

ACRL INFORMATION DIETARY STANDARDS ADDRESSED
Standard One: 1.2.

MAIN COOKING TECHNIQUE
Short presentation of concepts, learning game

MAIN INGREDIENTS
- Instruction station
- PowerPoint
- Computer workstations for students (individual or shared)
- Candy (a popular and easily obtainable motivation device)

PREPARATION
You will need to prepare PowerPoint slides with images of journal and magazine covers, and also screenshots of database citations, in random order, one image per slide.

THE INSTRUCTION SESSION
1. It is handy to have the presentation software up and minimized before starting. I normally begin with a short introductory sentence about Scholarly and Popular sources. I generally ask students to explain what it means, or what they think it means. Sometimes they do not know and so I explain briefly. Other times someone will know and explain for the class. In any case I give candy to those who answer.
2. Tell students that we will play an audience participation game to test their knowledge and understanding of this concept. If not using clickers, explain to them that you will flash images on the screen, and they need to clap to indicate if the item they are looking at is a popular journal, and to snap their fingers if the item is Scholarly/Peer-Reviewed. If clickers are used, have them turn them on and explain that they will be voting on each image.
3. Display each slide one at a time. Have students vote on each image. Pause after each vote to have a volunteer or randomly chosen students explain why they voted the way they did. Give candy to respondents.

ALLERGY WARNINGS
There are occasional groans, but candy appears to alleviate some of the grumpiness.

CHEF'S NOTE
I have done this often with classes, especially in those dreaded sessions where the professor has no assignment, or is absent. It is invariably energizing for students, and keeps their attention. When it goes off well it can be amusing, especially if the Librarian picks amusing or different periodical covers to display.

Internet Taste-Test: Evaluating Websites

In this recipe, students brainstorm criteria with which to evaluate Web sites.

Amanda K. Izenstark, Reference and Instructional Design Librarian, University of Rhode Island, Kingston, RI, amanda@uri.edu
Mary C. MacDonald, Head of Instruction, University of Rhode Island, Kingston, RI, marymac@uri.edu

NUTRITION INFORMATION
After students work in small groups to brainstorm criteria they could use to evaluate a Web site, the class discusses their findings. Small groups then evaluate individual Web sites.

COOKING TIME
Cooking time is 60 to 120 minutes and serves ten to forty students of any class level.

ACRL INFORMATION DIETARY STANDARDS ADDRESSED
Standard Three: 3.2, 3.6.

MAIN COOKING TECHNIQUE
Brainstorming, small group hands-on exploration of Web site features, small group reporting/presentations

MAIN INGREDIENTS
- Enough computers so students can comfortably work together in small groups
- Enough preselected Web sites to give each group two web sites to evaluate, URLs written in pairs on note cards for distribution.
- Internet Evaluation Worksheet (One copy for each small group.)

PREPARATION
- The Internet Evaluation Worksheet is a three-column table with the leftmost column for student-devised criteria, and a column for each Web site to record how it meets the criteria.
- Select a number of Web sites for students to compare and contrast.
- Copy paper handouts, or prepare online exercise in Course Management Software.

THE INSTRUCTION SESSION
1. **Brainstorming**—5-7 minutes.
   Small groups (two—three students) will brainstorm and/or devise criteria for evaluating the credibility and usefulness of Web sites.
2. **Discussing and sharing**—5 minutes.
   Groups report their criteria. Depending on the size of the class, ask each group to suggest one or two elements, rather than their entire list. If possible, note elements on a whiteboard.
3. **Exploring**—15-20 minutes.
   Distribute URLs and provide hands-on time to use criteria to evaluate their specific web site(s).

4. **Presenting and discussing**—20-25 minutes.
   Instructor facilitates discussion of sites and criteria. During the last few minutes of class ask students why it's important to evaluate information online.

ALLERGY WARNINGS
The internet is a volatile place; verify continued existence of web sites before session begins.

CHEF'S NOTE
- By adjusting the Web sites to meet the needs of the class, students were able to explore resources they hadn't been exposed to before, and to share their findings with their classmates.
- Web sites used may be a combination of general interest sites, subject-specific sites, hoax sites, and/or useful resources.
- WebCT, Blackboard, Sakai, or other course management software can be used instead of a paper handout and/or in person presentations.
- For shorter class periods, or to leave more time for discussion, give each group of students only one site.

Not All Web Sites Smell Bad—Infusing the Internet with the Essence of Evaluation

This recipe addresses a major bane of librarians in the new century—students who are unable to evaluate the quality of a website. This activity presents students with simple evaluative criteria. Smells aromatic in the classroom.

Allison Carr, Social Sciences Librarian, CSU San Marcos, acarr@csusm.edu

NUTRITION INFORMATION

Many freshmen and sophomores have trouble understanding how to decide if a Web site is appropriate to use for a college-level research paper. Students need a quick list of criteria they can use to evaluate a Web site, and they need to practice evaluating. Students work together to evaluate a Web site for authority, currency, purpose, and validity.

COOKING TIME

Cooking time is 50 to 75 minutes. Serves undergraduates in a class of twenty-five.

ACRL INFORMATION DIETARY STANDARDS ADDRESSED

Standard Three: 3.1, 3.3

MAIN COOKING TECHNIQUE

Jigsaw, Directed learning, small group activity, peer-teaching

MAIN INGREDIENTS

- Computers (can be one computer for two to three students)
- Worksheets

PREPARATION

Librarian should choose four to five Web sites for the students to evaluate based on the topic for their class. Prepare a worksheet including evaluative criteria.

THE INSTRUCTION SESSION

1. **Introduction**—10 minutes
   a. Break students into small groups
   b. Brief introduction to evaluating Web sites
   c. Class discusses the importance of evaluating websites to use in a college-level research paper
   d. Instructor reviews the criteria to evaluate each Web site (using the handout as a scaffold)
      i. Identity (meaning of URL)
      ii. Authority
      iii. Purpose
      iv. Validity/Reliability
      v. Currency
   e. Class reviews a sample Web site to practice

2. **Activity**—Practice Evaluating—20—30 minutes
   a. Assign each group a Web site to evaluate. I used sample Web sites based on a career discovery assignment. (These can be changed to fit your subject.)
      i. The Occupational Outlook Handbook online (http://www.bls.gov/OCO/)
      ii. A Yahoo news article related to a career

   iii. A professional organization related to a career
   iv. A scholarly article related to a career (found through Google, but available through the library)
   v. A Union Web site

3. **Activity**—Peer Teaching—10—15 minutes
   a. After each group has completed their evaluation, students regroup. Students do mini-presentation to their fellow small group members, teaching each other about their evaluations and what they have learned.

4. **Review**—10—15 minutes
   Instructor and class reviews Web sites together as a class discussion.

ALLERGY WARNINGS

Students may not really teach their classmates about the assignment, but instead regurgitate or copy their notes from their handouts. Avoid this by asking students to present their Web site, showing how and why they came to their conclusion.

CHEF'S NOTE

- One of my favorite things about this activity is that it is truly active learning. I briefly introduce the evaluation criteria and students have to dig deeper to answer the questions asked. When given enough time, students do find the answers to their own questions (e.g., "I really can't figure out what this Web site is, can you just tell me?").

- By asking them ahead of time to be prepared to teach it to their peers, they want to find the correct answers. This encourages students to think about how to explain their evaluations to their peers in a language they understand.

- This activity works best in extended sessions (or as part of multiple sessions), or in a workshop setting.

CABLE Cook-off: Learning to Evaluate Web Sites

This recipe helps undergraduates learn how to evaluate Web sites so they will know which ones are appropriate to cite for college-level papers and projects.

Christina Chester-Fangman, Instruction Librarian and Assistant Professor, Austin Peay State University, Clarksville, TN, chester-fangmanc@apsu.edu

NUTRITION INFORMATION

This recipe allows students who are relatively new to the research process to compare and contrast Web sites. Students choose Web sites and evaluate them in a group cook-off using CABLE criteria. The lesson can be incorporated into a variety of assignments, but it is especially useful to those who are preparing a persuasive speech or essay on a hot topic issue and need to find sources to support their arguments.

COOKING TIME

Cooking time is 55 minutes and serves twenty.

ACRL INFORMATION DIETARY STANDARDS ADDRESSED

Standard One: 1.1, 1.2.
Standard Two: 2.2, 2.4.
Standard Three: 3.2, 3.4.

MAIN COOKING TECHNIQUE

Mini-demonstration, small-group work, peer assistance, presentation

MAIN INGREDIENTS

- Computer access for all students
- Instructor station
- PowerPoint software for CABLE lesson
- CABLE worksheet

PREPARATION

Instructors should be familiar with the CABLE concept. Students should have already chosen their topics.

THE INSTRUCTION SESSION

1. Group students based upon their selected topics.
2. Explain CABLE to students—10 minutes.
   Present CABLE via PowerPoint, explaining to students what they need to look for in evaluating Web sites:
   C=Currency
   A=Authority
   B=Bias
   L=Level
   E=Explore!
3. Students work in groups—30 minutes.
   Students find Web sites to support their topics and answer the CABLE questions.
4. Groups present findings—5 minutes.

ALLERGY WARNINGS

- Ideally, the groups will be close to even in number. You may have to split larger groups into smaller, more manageable ones.
- Move around the room and among the groups to make sure every student is involved in the evaluative process. Be available to answer questions.

CHEF'S NOTE

- Many students think that it is appropriate for them to use any resources they find on the Web for their assignments. It is so important that the students explore: that they take their research to the next level to investigate, verify, and evaluate resources. This is a great opportunity for them to learn those essential analytical and critical thinking skills.
- CABLE logo designed by Gina Garber, Digital Services Librarian / Archivist and Assistant Professor, Austin Peay State University

CURRENCY—When was the page created? As best as you can tell, is the information up to date? Are links from this site to other sites still active?

AUTHORITY—Who is the author for each page? Are the credentials of the author listed? What is the domain name for the site and why is that relevant?

BIAS—What is the purpose of the site? Is there a position/opinion presented? What is it? Does this site link to any other sites? If yes, which ones?

LEVEL—Is this site popular or scholarly in nature? Do you feel comfortable citing this page in a college-level assignment? Why or why not?

EXPLORE!—Verify the information from the page in one additional source and list the source. Can you find reviews, criticism, or a ranking for this site? Does this site lead you to any other good sites? If so, list one or two.

Lettuce Help You Separate the Wheat from the Chaff! A Healthy Approach to Using the Web Effectively

This recipe begins with a discussion of the need for evaluating Web sites. Most of the session is then taken up with students reviewing Web sites and thinking about their potential for scholarship.

Nigel Morgan, Subject Librarian, Cardiff University, MorganNJ@cardiff.ac.uk
Linda Davies, Science and Biosciences Librarian, Cardiff University, DaviesL10@cf.ac.uk

NUTRITION INFORMATION

This recipe proposes to provide a highly practical introduction to the evaluation of Web information; build on the students' existing knowledge of using internet search engines; compare and contrast a range of themed Web sites according to a set of carefully defined criteria, e.g., author/source, authority, date/currency, design/layout; and apply these criteria while searching for and evaluating other sites which must meet the standards identified in the session.

COOKING TIME

Cooking time is 60—90 minutes and serves thirty Medicine/Biosciences students.

ACRL INFORMATION DIETARY STANDARDS ADDRESSED

Standard Three: 3.1, 3.2, 3.4.

MAIN COOKING TECHNIQUE

Hands-on practical work, discussion in pairs, group discussion, individual evaluative work using checklist

MAIN INGREDIENTS

- Computer access for all students
- A journal/newspaper article on the problems associated with tracing quality information on the Web
- URLs to at least three Web sites on an interesting or mildly controversial topic. We dished up a selection of sites on Vegetarianism including the site of the fabulous Lettuce Ladies, The Health Properties of Tomatoes, and Cloning
- Copies of a Web site evaluation checklist
- A Critique Sheet giving your own views/assessments of the evaluated sites

PREPARATION

Select a short, pithy article that covers the key points of the session. We chose a newspaper article that reported that a Professor had banned her first year students from using Google; and as an alternative, provided them with 200 peer-reviewed articles. Prepare your checklist of evaluation criteria or adapt an already existing one. Research the topics you are going to use and in each case select:

- a high-quality site, well-referenced, and from a reputable source
- a Web page of average quality, which is insufficiently referenced or in which there is the possibility of bias
- a Web site unsuitable for academic use; appropriate examples could include sites of bad design, sites containing poor quality information, or those of a frivolous or entertaining nature

If possible, create a Web page to give students easy access.

THE INSTRUCTION SESSION

1. **Introduction**
   a. Explain how training evolves from previous sessions (if applicable) and provide a quick general introduction to evaluating Web information
   b. Allocate 10 minutes or so for the students to read the article and to discuss their reaction in pairs

c. Initiate a general discussion, "What were the key points in the article?"

2. **Web site exploration**
   a. Ask students to explore the selected Web sites, and complete the checklist
   b. For each site, ask them to come to a considered conclusion, "Could you use the information with confidence in an academic piece of work?" Ask them to justify their decision

3. **More practice**
   a. Set additional task—Choose a site of which authorship is unclear. Ask students to play detective and discover who has provided the information

4. **Even more practice**
   a. Ask students to put the criteria into action by finding a high-quality site on a specific topic

5. **Conclusion**
   a. Towards the end of the session, hand out your Web site Critiques Sheets and ask the students to compare their responses to your own
   b. Finish by summing up the lessons learned and their implications for future searching

ALLERGY WARNINGS

- Ensure that the discussion article is succinct and clear.
- Students can be sidetracked by the content of the sites, so be prepared to move students on.
- Expect lots of questions when evaluating the Web sites; and make sure you've checked them out thoroughly beforehand.

CHEF'S NOTE

- This has proved an enjoyable and worthwhile way of getting students to ask crucial questions about the quality of the information they find. Some found the session a real eye-opener. For example, we asked students to find out who was the author/organisation behind the information on http://lycopene.org. This is a Web site devoted to the benefits of the antioxidant found in tomato-based products. This is not

made explicit on the site; however, e-mail contact details reveal that the site has been sponsored by Heinz, a leading manufacturer of tomato products. Once explained to the students, this throws a new light on the content of the site.

- This session is part of a series beginning with basic training on finding information in books and journals. The session can stand alone or the content can be integrated into a broader session covering other aspects of the Web, for example using search tools, referencing Web sources etc.
- The session can be extended with a referencing exercise, emphasising the practical application of the evaluation and underlining the quality message, i.e., "If you can't find sufficient details to cite it correctly, don't use it".

The Art of Choosing the Very Best Ingredients—Website Evaluation 101

This recipe will provide your students with the ingredients for evaluating a Web site.

Vivian Milczarski, Collection Development and Electronic Resources Librarian, Mount Saint Mary College, Newburgh, NY, milczars@msmc.edu; Jacqueline Ryan, Access Services Librarian, Mount Saint Mary College, Newburgh, NY, jryan@msmc.edu

NUTRITION INFORMATION

This recipe will provide students with the opportunity to learn to distinguish between Good and Bad Web sites. It will also give students the opportunity to work together with peers in small groups, and allow the students to share their discoveries with the class.

Ingredients for Evaluating a Web Site
- Combine 1 part each:
  o Authority
  o Accuracy
  o Objectivity
  o Currency
  o Coverage
- Add a pinch of skepticism
- Stir briskly and use wisely

COOKING TIME

Cooking time is 60—90 minutes and serves a class of thirty freshmen.

ACRL INFORMATION DIETARY STANDARDS ADDRESSED

Standard One: 1.1
Standard Two: 2.2, 2.3, 2.4
Standard Three: 3.2, 3.4.

MAIN COOKING TECHNIQUE

Mini-demonstration, small-group work

MAIN INGREDIENTS

- Computer access for all students
- Instructor station

PREPARATION

- List of Web site examples
- PowerPoint to illustrate the criteria for evaluating Web resources.
- Potential topics for students to use, if necessary.
- Group worksheet

Lenon the Literary Lion

THE INSTRUCTION SESSION

1. **Introduction**—10 minutes.
   a. Briefly review assignment with class.
   b. Remind them that they have had an overview of library resources in a previous session.
   c. Do a PowerPoint mini-lecture and demonstration about the difference between the authoritative information found in library databases vs. information found on the Web. Stress that the focus of today's class will be to provide them with tools, techniques, and criteria to evaluate Web sites effectively. Explain that we will be using *Autism* and *Vaccinations* as a sample topic to research. Briefly review evaluation criteria by providing an overview of two Web sites on the topic.
      i. Centers for Disease Control—http://CDC.gov/vaccinesafety
      ii. National Vaccine Information Center—http://www.nvic.org//
2. **Group activity**—25 minutes.

a. Have students break into groups and choose a topic to research (no more than 5 minutes). Circulate to answer questions and help students identify fruitful topics.

b. Allow groups 15-20 minutes to search chosen topics and prepare to briefly share their findings with the group. Students will be asked to quickly evaluate Web sites and try to identify at least one unbiased/authoritative site as well as at least one suspect or biased site.

3. **Groups report**—20 minutes.

a. Instructors will ask for volunteer presenters to share their findings with the group. If no volunteers come forward, a lucky group will be chosen by the instructors!

4. **Conclusion**

a. Review the main concepts of Web site evaluation, stress that this is an ongoing process which will require practice, and allow students to comment on their discoveries while doing this exercise.

ALLERGY WARNINGS

Students may not be eager to research a topic that does not interest them; hopefully each group will be able to reach consensus and join together in a common purpose.

CHEF'S NOTE

• We greatly enjoyed facilitating this workshop. We prepared a PowerPoint presentation with screen captures representing four of our criteria for evaluating internet resources. These screen captures proved very valuable in terms of keeping the instruction focused and brief. We used the slides to highlight an authoritative site, the Centers for Disease Control and prevention (http://CDC.gov) and a more biased site, the National Vaccine Information Center, (http://www.nvic.org//).

• Our students were engaged and worked diligently together. They obviously liked sleuthing through Web sites in search of the "Who we are" or "About" section. Some groups went more deeply into the authoritative sites; others found an authoritative AND a biased site for effective comparison.

• At the end of the group work portion, we asked for a few examples of topics chosen and we projected a couple of the Web sites on the screen for group discussion. The students were very animated during this part of the workshop since it involved group participation rather than straight lecture.

• Overall, this was a very positive experience that strengthened our instructional skills. And according to the feedback we received, it greatly benefited the students who participated.

5. SPECIALIZED RESEARCH SKILLS

Cooking with the Past: A Hands-On Approach to Interpreting Primary Sources

This recipe gives students the actual experience of working with original materials. Students examine an item and answer a series of critical questions.

James Gerencser, Archives and Special Collections, Dickinson College, gerencse@dickinson.edu
Malinda Triller, Archives and Special Collections, Dickinson College, trillerm@dickinson.edu

NUTRITION INFORMATION

In today's easy-access digital world, students are generally unfamiliar with how information was communicated in the past, what those forms of communication looked like, and how original documents can enhance their own understanding of a particular person or event. This recipe is designed to encourage an awareness and appreciation of the value of primary source materials. Students will demonstrate the ability to extract information from original documents.

COOKING TIME

Cooking time is 45 to 75 minutes and serves twenty students.

ACRL INFORMATION DIETARY STANDARDS ADDRESSED

Standard One: 1.2
Standard Three: 3.1, 3.2.

MAIN COOKING TECHNIQUE

Hands-on, individual document analysis, group discussion

MAIN INGREDIENTS

Collect historical documents, photographs, or artifacts that represent a wide range of formats, functions, and points-of-view. Be sure to select materials that may be of particular interest to the students, that may help to tell interesting stories, or that are somehow connected to larger events.

PREPARATION

- Gather the primary sources, ideally one for each student.
- Prepare a list of document analysis questions to distribute to each student (optional).

THE INSTRUCTION SESSION

1. **Individual artifact examination**—10 minutes
   a. Distribute an original document to each member of the class and ask the students to take a few minutes to study their items as they keep in mind the following questions:
      i. What type of document do you have (letter, photograph, ledger, etc.)?
      ii. Who created the document?
      iii. When was it created?
      iv. Who was the intended audience?
      v. What function did the document serve?
      vi. What information can you learn from this and similar documents?
      vii. How does this document compare to modern sources of information?
   b. While the students are examining their documents, circulate among them to answer any questions they may have and to help them interpret information and forms of documentation that may be unfamiliar to them.

2. Group discussion

a. Ask each student to describe his or her document to the rest of the class and to answer the questions listed above.

b. Encourage students to think about how their individual documents relate to each other by comparing and contrasting them. For example, do some students have documents that deal with a common issue but differ in format, purpose, or content?

c. Initiate discussion about how document format, intended audience, point-of-view, and date of creation influence the type of information and evidence a primary resource might provide.

3. Conclusion

a. Conclude the class by asking the students to consider other questions their documents might help to answer and how they might make use of them in their own research.

ALLERGY WARNINGS

• Some students may have difficulty identifying and interpreting documents in formats that are unfamiliar to them (e.g. formal correspondence, memoranda, etc.) and they may need gentle prompting or guidance from the instructor to help them understand their documents.

• Students will often get bogged down trying to read every word and discern every detail. When circulating among them, try to keep them focused on the questions that you posed and help them to think more broadly.

• Students generally struggle with handwritten documents, especially those containing older styles of script. Try to select handwritten documents that will not be too difficult to read, or else provide printed transcriptions alongside the original documents.

CHEF'S NOTE

• This activity is an adaptation of the traditional written document analysis assignment. The advantage of engaging in this activity as a group is that students are exposed to a wide variety of primary sources and can start to see how people communicated information differently in the past. Through this activity, students can also begin making connections between various types of sources. Students are able to make these connections more easily if the instructor consciously selects documents that have some element in common, such as topic, function, author, etc.

• Students are most engaged in this activity and find it more relevant if the documents relate to a topic addressed in the course or are potentially useful for research assignments in the course.

• Copies of documents can be used to protect fragile materials, but this activity has more of an impact if students can handle the originals.

• We have used this activity on a regular basis in Historical Research Methods courses for several years with very good results. We find that students become actively engaged when provided an opportunity to handle original historic materials.

Annotated Bibliographies: The Good, The Bad, and The...Tasty?

In this recipe students compare a well-written annotation to one which is poorly written. From these examples, students determine criteria of a good annotation.

Sara R. Seely, Reference and Instruction Librarian, Boise State University, saraseely@boisestate.edu

NUTRITION INFORMATION
This recipe is intended for undergraduate students who have been asked to prepare an annotated bibliography as part of their coursework. The students articulate the qualities of a good annotation and apply these criteria to their own work.

COOKING TIME
Cooking time is 50 to 70 minutes and serves no more than thirty students.

ACRL INFORMATION DIETARY STANDARDS ADDRESSED
Standard Three: 3.1, 3.2, 3.3, 3.4
Standard Four: 4.1, 4.2, 4.3
Standard Five: 5.3.

MAIN COOKING TECHNIQUE
Small group collaborative exercise, individual exercises, group discussion

MAIN INGREDIENTS
- White board for recording group discussion
- Each student brings an article to annotate

PREPARATION
Create a worksheet with two sample annotations, providing one as an exemplary annotation and one that needs improvement.

THE INSTRUCTION SESSION
1. Each student receives two sample annotations.
2. **Individual work**—5 minutes
   Determine which is the Good annotation and which is the Bad annotation
3. **Small group work**—5 minutes
   Students discuss their findings
4. **Class discussion**—10 minutes
   a. Determine the qualities of a good annotation
      i. it summarizes the source material
      ii. it paraphrases the source material
      iii. it explains how the article fits into the general literature on the subject
   b. Discuss criteria until there is consensus.
5. **Individual work**—10 minutes
   Now have students work individually to practice annotating the article they brought with them.
6. **Small group work**—20–40 minutes

Finally, students take turns in their group sharing their annotation and getting feedback from group mates.

ALLERGY WARNINGS
When writing the example annotations, it's good to choose a topic relevant to the course subject and include some of the key mistakes, such as exaggerations or quoting without citing.

CHEF'S NOTE
Students seem to appreciate the opportunity to practice writing annotations if it is a key part of their course work. I have feedback from instructors that students' work has improved after this practice session.

"X" Marks the Spot: Using Concept Maps to Find Hidden Treasures

This recipe will show students an easier way to brainstorm and choose topics by working with a concept map.

Emaly Conerly, Carson-Newman College, econerly@cn.edu
Kelli Williams, Carson-Newman College, kwilliams@cn.edu

NUTRITION INFORMATION
Concept maps correspond nicely with database research (especially subject searching), and can help students explore new areas and ideas with ease.

COOKING TIME
Cooking time is 60 minutes and typically serves twenty students.

ACRL INFORMATION DIETARY STANDARDS ADDRESSED
Standard One: 1.1, 1.2, 1.3, 1.4.
Standard Two: 2.1, 2.2, 2.3, 2.4, 2.5.
Standard Three: 3.1, 3.2, 3.3, 3.4, 3.5, 3.6, 3.7.
Standard Four: 4.1, 4.2, 4.3.

MAIN COOKING TECHNIQUE
Worksheets, group discussion, hands-on

MAIN INGREDIENTS
- Computer lab
- Handouts for class; should contain general Library information, list of relevant databases, and two concept maps (one already filled in and one left blank)

PREPARATION
Print handouts for each student

THE INSTRUCTION SESSION
1. Explain goal for session. Point to the Library's home page on the instructor's screen
2. Give instructions—
   a. Spend a couple of minutes discussing general Library information on the handout (contact information, hours, where links may be found on the homepage, etc.)
   b. Show the students where to find the online databases
   c. Discuss the completed concept map, explaining the process and its usefulness
3. Have each student enter into the database you choose, and let them conduct subject or subject guide searches to find the information they need for their own concept map

ALLERGY WARNINGS
- Some students may need additional help evaluating and processing the information they find
- Check for errors and problem areas in the students' work—help them as necessary

CHEFS' NOTE
- Some students are more adept than others in interpreting their search results
- The professors have given very positive feedback on this session
- This is a great way to reinforce the value of subject searching and evaluating subject terms to help develop and refine research topics

Cooking up Concept Maps

Concept maps allow students to visually work through an idea for potentially useful search terms.

Abigail Hawkins, Instructional Designer, abbyhawkins7@gmail.com; Jennifer Fabbi, Head, Curriculum Materials Library and Special Assistant to the Dean, University of Nevada, Las Vegas Libraries, jennifer.fabbi@unlv.edu; and Paula McMillen, Education Librarian, University of Nevada, Las Vegas Libraries, paula.mcmillen@unlv.edu

NUTRITION INFORMATION

A common roadblock students experience in the research process is identifying central concepts in their research questions and devising useful ways to reframe search terms. Concept mapping is one instructional strategy that can be used to help students better identify the central concepts in their research questions and expand on other ways these concepts are articulated in the literature.

COOKING TIME

Cooking time is dependent upon the particular application.

ACRL INFORMATION DIETARY STANDARDS ADDRESSED

Standard One: 1.1.e, 1.1.c
Standard Two: 2.2.b

MAIN COOKING TECHNIQUE

Individual reflection, work in pairs, and large group discussion

MAIN INGREDIENTS

Whiteboard /Blackboard or instructor's station with projector

PREPARATION

In advance of the session, students will have identified a manageable research question, which their instructor will have approved.

THE INSTRUCTION SESSION

1. **Introduce self and gain attention**—5 minutes
    Share a personal story where you were looking for information on a given research question and had difficulty finding it. For example, searching for information on *students being held back a grade*, but finding it is indexed as *grade repetition*.

2. **State the purpose of the session**—1 minute
    Identify main concepts of your research question and develop alternate terms (synonyms, broader/narrower, or related terms) for your concepts to facilitate searching.

Student Worksheet

Create a concept map.

- Central circle: Your research question
- Secondary circles: Main concepts from your research question
- Boxes: Alternate terms (synonyms, broader/narrower, or related terms) for each concept.

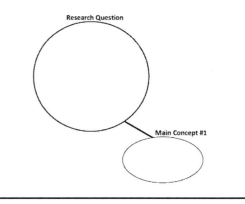

3. **Introduce the concept map**—1 minute
    A strategy students can use to help them think through their research questions before starting to search.

4. **Model creating a concept map and have students create their own simultaneously**—25 minutes
Identify main concepts: Create a large circle on the whiteboard. Write your main question in the center circle. Ask students to identify the main concepts of this research question. Draw circles extending off of the research question with one main concept per circle.
    i. Give students three minutes to start their own concept map and identify the main concepts of their research question. Roam the room providing help as needed.
  b. Identify alternate terms: Restate that one of your problems in searching initially was that you fixated on a specific term and did not think to search using a different word. Ask students to come up with alternate terms (synonyms, broader/narrower, or related terms) for each main concept that you could have searched under to have had more success finding information. Draw boxes extending off the main concepts with one term per square.
  c. Give students five minutes to identify alternate terms (synonyms, broader/narrower, or related terms) for each of their main concepts. Roam the room providing assistance as needed

  d. Have students share their maps with their peers and give suggestions of alternate terms.

ALLERGY WARNINGS
It is important that the instructors give students feedback on their research questions in advance. This ensures that the concept map will be relevant when students begin searching for information.

CHEFS' NOTE
You can leverage the concept map to introduce, model, and practice Boolean logic if desired (main concepts use AND connectors and synonymous concepts use OR connectors).

The strategy can be used as pre-work for a more substantial research inquiry. See *Whipping up the "Why" Paper* in Section 6.

A different way you can use concept mapping is as a brainstorming tool to help students explore a research topic with the purpose of identifying a research question.

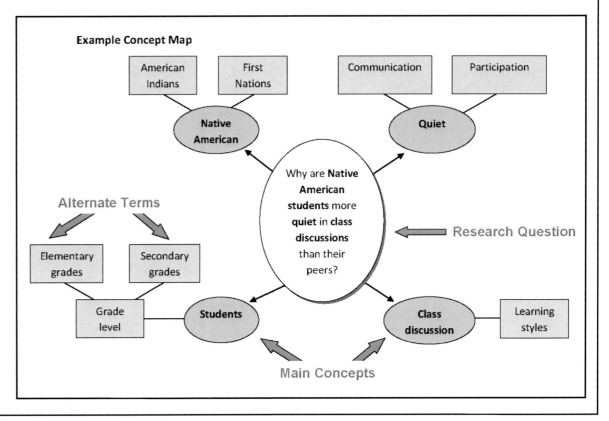

Example Concept Map

Database du Jour

This recipe models information-seeking behavior. Students analyze and compare databases in order to learn to which is best for their needs.

Theresa Westbrock, Instruction Coordinator, New Mexico State University Library, twestbro@nmsu.edu

NUTRITION INFORMATION
The purpose of this recipe is to have students explore and evaluate various databases before they use them to search for information. This recipe will teach students to learn to choose appropriate databases for their research interests.

COOKING TIME
Cooking time is 60-minutes.

ACRL INFORMATION DIETARY STANDARDS ADDRESSED
Standard One: 1.1
Standard Two: 2.2

MAIN COOKING TECHNIQUE
Discussion, collaborative demonstration

MAIN INGREDIENTS
- Computer lab
- Teaching station
- Database evaluation handouts

PREPARATION
There is little preparation needed for this lesson. Choose a database to use for the sample evaluation. I have two different strategies. Use a general-interest database (Academic Search Premier or InfoTrac OneFile) since most students will be at least familiar with them. Or use a subject-specific database so that you can show the importance of identifying the publisher, thesaurus, etc. It is helpful to fill in the handout to be used as the sample in class.

THE INSTRUCTION SESSION
1. **Introduction**
   a. Briefly explain the purpose of the session. Introduce library databases to students. Define some of the related language: index, thesaurus, controlled language, etc.
   b. Ask students questions such as
      i. What do you know about library databases?
      ii. What databases do you use? Why?
      iii. Have you ever used _____ database? Why or why not?
      iv. Why do you think there are so many databases?

2. **Group evaluation**
   a. Give the students the database evaluation handout.
   b. As a group, have students help you fill out the evaluation form. Guide them, but make them find the answers. As you move from category to category, discuss why each is important.

3. **Individual hands-on evaluation**
   a. Have students evaluate two databases on their own (or in groups of two, depending on the class dynamics).

4. **Final discussion**
   a. When students have finished, ask them questions such as
      i. Why are there so many databases?
      ii. Why is it important to evaluate a database before you use it?
      iii. What would be a good database to use if looking for _____?
      iv. What surprised you when looking at the different databases?

ALLERGY WARNINGS

This class is much more relevant to students who have a major area of academic interest. Students are usually thrilled to find the variety of information collected in different databases.

CHEF'S NOTE

- I use this recipe often. Students tend to use the databases they are familiar with, and rarely explore other resources on their own. Plus, students find this lesson empowering. I often hear some version of, "I wish I would have known about _____ last year!"

- I think it is important for us, as librarians, to model our information-seeking behavior to students. This recipe does not tell students which databases to use, nor does it tell students that the way they are doing things is wrong. It gives them an opportunity to explore, in a guided fashion, resources that we know they will find useful. And this recipe puts the responsibility on the student.

- This recipe is also very successful when followed by an advanced search techniques session.

Database Evaluation Sheet		1.	2.	3.
Name of database:				
Publisher	*e.g. APA, MLA, USDA*			
Vendor	*e.g. Ebsco, Proquest, CSA*			
Subject of material	*What topic(s) or discipline(s) are covered?*			
Type of material	*News articles? Journal articles? Books? Proceedings? etc.*			
Time coverage	*How far back is coverage?*			
Update schedule	*How recently updated?*			
Abstracts?	*y/n*			
Full Text? Format?	*y/n pdf? html?*			
Exportable records?	*y/n*			
Other	*Access, ease of use, subject headings, thesaurus, extra features, tips/tricks, truncation rules, pros/cons*			

Developing a Taste for Government Documents
This recipe introduces students to the value of government documents as primary sources.

Lauren Jensen, Public Services Librarian, Hewes Library, Monmouth College, Monmouth, Illinois, ljensen@monm.edu
Lynn Daw, Technical Services Librarian, Hewes Library, Monmouth College, Monmouth, Illinois, ldaw@monm.edu

NUTRITION INFORMATION
This recipe was developed to introduce students to the breadth and nature of government information. It also allows for student collaboration and provides an opportunity for students to refine their research skills.

COOKING TIME
Cooking time is 60 minutes. Serves twenty to twenty-five students.

ACRL INFORMATION DIETARY STANDARDS ADDRESSED
Standard One: 1.1, 1.2, 1.3
Standard Two: 2.1, 2.2, 2.3, 2.4, 2.5
Standard Three: 3.2, 3.4, 3.7

MAIN COOKING TECHNIQUE
Small group work, short demonstrations, peer collaboration

MAIN INGREDIENTS
- Computer lab
- Proximity to print Government Documents is a plus

PREPARATION
Before the students arrive, familiarize yourself with key resources and the historical time period to be researched.

THE INSTRUCTION SESSION
1. **Introduction**
   a. Begin with a short introduction of the goals of the session.
   b. Provide a short demonstration of where and how to locate government information in the library. We include both print and online resources.
2. **Small group research**
   a. Pairs of students work to locate resources on their paper's topic, keeping track of their steps and results.
   b. Allow students to leave classroom to retrieve resources.
   c. While students are working, circulate among them to answer questions and provide direction. It is helpful, although not necessary, to have more than one librarian available to assist students.
3. **Report back to class**
   a. Near the end of class, have one representative from each group share the group's results.

ALLERGY WARNINGS
Many students do not realize that the U.S. Government is a large publisher of paper and online materials. Students can be overwhelmed.

CHEF'S NOTE
Every time we teach this instruction session, students are amazed to learn the value of government information. Students willingly stay after class to look for more resources or refine their searches after the initial investigation is underway.

Many of these instruction sessions have led to individual consultations and lifelong library supporters.

A Scoop of New with a Dash of Review! Using Bibliographic Management Software

This recipe tantalizes graduate students with instruction on EndNote and advice on managing large library research projects.

Dee Bozeman, Regional Campus Librarian, University of Central Florida, Daytona State College/UCF Joint-Use Library, Daytona Beach, dbozeman@mail.ucf.edu

NUTRITION INFORMATION

This recipe uses EndNote, a bibliographic management software package, to pique the taste buds of graduate students. As well as being a re-acquaintance with library resources, the recipe also helps graduate students to familiarize themselves with the creation and management of a large research project.

COOKING TIME

Cooking time is two hours minimum and serves ten to fifteen graduate students.

ACRL INFORMATION DIETARY STANDARDS ADDRESSED

Standard One: 1.2
Standard Two: 2.1, 2.2, 2.3, 2.4, 2.5
Standard Three: 3.3, 3.5

MAIN COOKING TECHNIQUE

Mini-demonstrations, individual work, peer assistance, librarian assistance

MAIN INGREDIENTS

- EndNote and Word on all the computers
- Each student needs a flash drive

PREPARATION

This session requires a working knowledge of EndNote and a familiarity with the resources available in the subject area.

THE INSTRUCTION SESSION

1. **Introduction**
   a. Present a quick overview of End-Note
   b. Demonstrate setting up a library in EndNote on a flash drive
2. **Hands-on**
   a. Demonstrate a search of one of the standard databases in the student's subject area
   b. Work with students having problems with searches
   c. Students practice exporting citation(s) to EndNote
   d. Review research tips and techniques as needed
   e. Repeat with a second database

3. **Using EndNote with Word**
   a. Demonstrate formatting bibliographies and Cite While You Write
   b. Students practice
4. **Conclusion**
   a. Save time for question

ALLERGY WARNINGS

Students may have had a library instruction class at the beginning of their program but that does not mean they remember searching techniques.

CHEF'S NOTE

This class gives the students a chance to work on their research, interact with peers, and have a librarian available for questions. Sometimes before I added EndNote to the class I would get complaints that the information had been covered in the previous session. Since they are learning about and using EndNote the students do not think of this as a refresher session on resources available and research skills. This is a really enjoyable class to work with since the students are very motivated.

Eating Forbidden Fruit: Censorship, Intellectual Freedom, and Banned Books

This recipe engages students with actual case studies to emphasize the complexities of this issue.

Nicole A. Cooke, Montclair State University, Reference and Instruction Librarian/Assistant Professor, Nicole.A.Cooke@gmail.com

NUTRITION INFORMATION
Graduate students in a Young Adult Literature course visit the library to learn about banned books, censorship, and intellectual freedom. By engaging with actual case studies, students learn about the complexities of this issue.

COOKING TIME
Cooking time is 60—90 minutes and serves twenty-five to thirty graduate students (typically practicing teachers).

ACRL INFORMATION DIETARY STANDARDS ADDRESSED
Standard Three: 3.3, 3.4, 3.5, 3.6
Standard Four: 4.1
Standard Five: 5.1

MAIN COOKING TECHNIQUE
Brief presentation, group exercises, group discussion

MAIN INGREDIENTS
- Handouts (optional); copies of banned books (optional).
- Instructional Resources and Handouts: In addition to examples from newspapers and periodicals, most of my information is obtained from ALA:
  - Banned Books Week graphics and materials
  - ALA press releases
  - The Most Frequently Challenged Books lists
  - ALA Office of Intellectual Freedom essays, position statements and newsletters
  - Banned Book challenge database form
  - Further reading list

PREPARATION
- Creation of two brief PowerPoints (Ban that Book! and Intellectual Freedom in the Library)
- Compilation of Ban that Book! exercise sheet
- Compilation of censorship case studies
- Creation of handouts

THE INSTRUCTION SESSION
1. **Introduction**
   a. After introducing myself and telling them what we will be discussing, I briefly explain the concepts of banned and challenged books.
2. **Ban that Book!** 15 minutes
   a. Students are broken into groups and are each given a list of books (titles, cover photos, and summaries).
   b. In 5 minutes, the groups must determine which, if any, of the books have been banned, and why.
   c. When the group reconvenes, each group presents their choices and rationales; this is accompanied by a PowerPoint, indicating which books have been banned and why. This process takes another 5-10 minutes.

3. **Censorship and intellectual freedom explanation**—10 minutes
   a. We go through another Power-Point with definitions and explanations of ALA's Banned Books Week, censorship, and intellectual freedom.
4. **Group work with case studies**—30 minutes
   a. The students are given a series of handouts and are briefed on the packet's contents.
   b. Finally, the students are again broken into groups and given a case study detailing an instance of censorship in libraries or schools. Their task is to think about how they would respond to the situation in question.
   c. After 10-15 minutes, the entire group reconvenes and reports out. Class-wide discussion takes a minimum of 10-15 minutes, but could extend much longer.

ALLERGY WARNINGS

- Depending on the dynamics of the group, the instructor must be comfortable ending groups' discussions and moving the class along and keeping on time. Conversely, if the class is not engaged (which I have not yet encountered) the instructor needs to be comfortable providing censorship examples and eliciting responses and experiences.
- Also, I have experienced strong reactions to some of the censorship examples I provide. I have to make it clear that we are not judging or debating specific issues. Instead, we are discussing documented instances of perceived censorship, as they occur with books, art, and other forms of media.

CHEF'S NOTE

- If possible, I would like more time for this session, as the conversations and discussions are always enlightening for the students and the instructors.
- Over time, I have reduced the number of handouts I provide. In the future, I will be developing a class blog to house materials, encourage discussion, and incorporate various Web 2.0 technologies.
- I have offered this session regularly over four years and have never had a class not fully engage in discussion.

However, I have had students become upset and overly passionate about examples of censorship, and it takes diplomacy and calm to diffuse such situations.

- Engage with the course instructor as much as possible before and during the session.
- Although the conversation may not be as in-depth as it tends to be with graduate students, this session could very well be presented to undergraduates.
- This is the most successful, interesting, and interactive class that I teach. This interactive group discussion format is thought provoking and is the best way I've found to engage the students.

Research Your Way Past Writer's Block

Advanced students often know the basics on how to use the library, but they need research support. This recipe helps graduate students to build a scholarly community.

Melissa Bowles-Terry, University of Illinois at Urbana–Champaign, mbowles2@illinois.edu
Merinda Hensley, University of Illinois at Urbana–Champaign, mhensle1@illinois.edu

NUTRITION INFORMATION

This is a recipe for students conducting a lengthy research project: senior thesis, master's thesis, or doctoral dissertation. Academic research and writing can be a very lonely affair. This workshop will provide students with:

- a scholarly community in which to share research woes and help solve each others' problems
- a chance to get help with research issues that they're stuck on
- tips on how to keep research organized over the course of an advanced project
- a venue for finding further research help in the library (e.g. connecting students with a subject specialist, locations of special collections, etc.)

COOKING TIME

Cooking time is at least 60 minutes and serves no more than twenty students.

ACRL INFORMATION DIETARY STANDARDS ADDRESSED

Standard One: 1.1, 1.4
Standard Four: 4.2

MAIN COOKING TECHNIQUE

Small group discussion, write/pair/share

MAIN INGREDIENTS

- Computer access for all students
- Blackboard/Whiteboard
- A copy of *Getting Things Done: The Art of Stress-Free Productivity* by David Allen. New York: Viking, 2001.

PREPARATION

- Have students pre-register and include the college in which they're studying.
- Prepare a list-making handout for students to create three lists: list of projects (long-term and short-term), to-do list, list of reminders of actions needed from others (things to follow-up on).
- Prepare to advise students on organizational strategies and tools.

THE INSTRUCTION SESSION

1. **Write**—5 minutes
   a. As students come into the class, they will do a Brain Dump.
   b. Instructions: sit down at a computer and start a list of your current research woes—the things that are keeping you up at night over your research project.
2. **Introductions**—5 minutes
   a. Name, department, subject of research (in a sentence or less!)
3. **Pair and share**—15 minutes
   a. Students form small groups, based on academic disciplines, and share their current research issues and discuss ways to address those issues.
   b. As students discuss, librarian roves, noting common themes and issues and joining conversations to give suggestions on solving research problems.
4. **Report**—20 minutes
   a. Groups give two-minute reports on common issues in their groups
      i. Share problem (e.g., navigating a particular database, having too much information, having too narrow a research topic)
      ii. Report on potential solutions

iii. Get feedback from class and librarian on how else to solve this problem

5. **Mini-lecture**—5 minutes

a. Librarian and graduate assistant offer tools for keeping research organized. Lightning fast introduction to *Getting Things Done* list-making method for staying on task.

i. List of projects—long-term projects, both academic and personal

ii. List of reminders for next actions (to do list)—physical actions that you need to do next to make your projects progress

iii. List of reminders of things you're waiting for from others (like e-mail responses, feedback from professors, etc.)

6. **Guided practice**—5 minutes

a. Handout with three list categories for students to start list-making. Students may start on this in class, but will take it with them to adapt to their own needs

7. **Conclusion:** When in need of assistance, don't hesitate to ask

ALLERGY WARNINGS

- Workshop must be publicized and marketed well in advance
- Students may need sample research issues to address before they start conversation. Otherwise, they may wander into territory that librarians may have a harder time addressing—difficult or unavailable advisor, lack of funding, etc. Try to stay focused on research and organization issues.
- Sample research issues:
  - Too much information on the topic—information overload
  - Navigating a particular database
  - Where to find some necessary information on the topic
  - How to re-find something you found once and can't relocate
  - How to stay on schedule with research/writing
  - How to keep track of all the journal articles, books, etc.
  - How to find out what's being published right now on the topic
- One of the issues we've dealt with most often in this workshop is current awareness. Students are often interested in learning how to set up RSS feeds, Table of Contents alerts, and the like in order to streamline the literature review process. Be prepared to show students some tools (RSS readers and database alerts) that they can use to stay abreast of new information on their thesis/dissertation topics.

CHEFS' NOTE

- This workshop fills a real need for graduate students who have been working in isolation and just need to talk through some of their research issues and get some fresh ideas on staying organized and completing a research project. As discussion facilitator, the librarian may feel at times like a therapist, listening to and sympathizing with research problems. More can happen, though, than just a gripe session.
- In one session of this workshop, a doctoral student mourned the loss of a citation that he found once but could never find again—"the one that got away." Fellow workshop attendees recalled their own sad stories of lost articles. The library instructor demonstrated the magic of Advanced Search in Google Scholar for finding partial citations. Later that week, the student sent a grateful e-mail to share the good news—the lost citation was found!
- In another workshop session, a student expressed a need for resources to translate a small but essential document for his research. A fellow student knew someone who would be able to perform that service and a deal was made!

Haiku, Self-Reflection, and the Research Process

Graduate students are asked to write a haiku about their research. This recipe is designed to help students think creatively (and metaphorically) about their topics.

Thomas Scott Duke, Associate Professor of Education, University of Alaska Southeast, Juneau, AK, thomas.duke@uas.alaska.edu
Jennifer Diane Ward (formerly Brown), Outreach Services Librarian and Assistant Professor of Library Science, University of Alaska Southeast, Juneau, AK, jennifer.ward@uas.alaska.edu

NUTRITION INFORMATION

Graduate students in our university's distance-delivered teacher education program are required to conduct a master's thesis project. Students design and conduct this research project while enrolled in a two-semester graduate seminar co-taught by an education faculty and an academic librarian. After our students select their research topics, we ask them to write a haiku poem that expresses their thoughts and feelings about their project. We also ask them to write a brief reflective paper that explains the meaning of their haiku.

Photo by: Ward F. Ward

COOKING TIME

Cooking time for this activity is 60 to 120 minutes serves no more than twenty graduate students.

ACRL INFORMATION DIETARY STANDARDS ADDRESSED

Standard One
Standard Three

MAIN COOKING TECHNIQUE

Lecture, peer learning, student presentations, class discussion

MAIN INGREDIENTS

- Access to the course Web site and electronic discussion board
- Sample haiku (written by the course instructors and by previous students)

PREPARATION

- Post instructions and sample haiku to the course website.
- Set up a forum in the course electronic discussion board where students will post their haiku and reflective papers and comment on their classmates' work.

**Self-reflection is
a recipe for success
haiku and research**

THE INSTRUCTION SESSION

1. Explain what a haiku is, providing samples.
2. Ask students to write a haiku about their research topic as homework.
3. Ask students to write a one to two page reflective paper that describes the meaning of their haiku.
4. Ask students to post haiku and reflective papers to electronic discussion board.
5. Ask students to read haiku and reflective papers written by at least two classmates and post comments on their classmates' work to electronic discussion board.
6. Students will present their haiku (via audio-conference) to the entire class at next class meeting.
7. Provide opportunities for class discussion (via audio-conference) after each student's presentation.

ALLERGY WARNINGS

Some students complain that they "are not very creative" and are unable to write poetry. Other students do not see the connection between creative writing (and creative thinking) and the research process.

CHEFS' NOTE

Thomas: Some students begin our course with misconceptions about the research process and their own roles as researchers. Initially, many of our students view themselves as passive consumers of other people's knowledge. I want our students to understand that research can (and should) be an intensely creative activity. Research does involve rigorous scholarship, but it should also involve self-reflection and self-expression on the part of the researcher. Compelling social science research informs, but it should also inspire. This activity helps students connect their own values, beliefs, interests, and experiences to their research projects—they begin to see themselves as active participants in the generation of new knowledge forms. This activity empowers our students by giving them permission to be creative and to step outside of their preconceived (and, often, very limited) notions of what research can and should be. Many of our students embed their haiku in the final version of their thesis reports as a way to illuminate important themes. They often use phrases from their haiku in the titles of their thesis reports. Many students identify keywords and phrases in their reflective papers and translate these words and phrases into search terms; they then use these search terms to conduct advanced database searches. Our students use these same keywords and phrases to reformulate and refine their research questions.

Jennifer: This recipe was inspired by a self-reflection activity in Valerie Janesick's text *"Stretching" Exercises for Qualitative Researchers* (Thousand Oaks, CA: Sage Publications, 2004). I really enjoy introducing this activity and seeing the results. The 5-7-5 form of haiku really helps students meditate on their research topics and sum up their essential thoughts on their projects. Many times students will do a series of haiku, rather than just one. The reflective paper on the haiku gives students a chance to get down their thoughts and ideas on the topic and it is a good place to start in the sometimes difficult process of narrowing a research topic.

Student: Johanna Tennant
Program: M.Ed. in Special Education, University of Alaska Southeast
Research Topic: Potential impact of differences in values, languages, and customs that can exist between the home and school.

**It's hard to teach a
Curriculum to Natives
Full of dead white men**

Student: Connie Phillips
Program: M.Ed. in Special Education, University of Alaska Southeast
Research Topic: Typical and atypical human growth and development.

**Defined before birth
Development arrested
Alcohol abuse**

Student: Sandy Dunkle
Program: M.Ed. in Special Education, University of Alaska Southeast
Research Topic: Family systems and the role of families in the educational process.

**Students' behavior
Reflect the home and family
Teachers be aware**

The Sous Chef Takes Center Stage: Using Experienced Students to Teach Their Classmates

This recipe makes use of peer instruction to teach students effective database searching techniques.

Veronica Arellano, Psychology and Social Work Librarian, University of Houston, Texas, varellano@gmail.com

NUTRITION INFORMATION

Students in a Psychology course are asked to develop a research proposal on a topic of their choosing. Their proposal must include a literature review of scholarly, peer-reviewed journal articles. Before beginning their literature review research, students attend a library instruction session to learn about research resources in Psychology, specifically the PsycINFO database.

The students in this course range from sophomores to seniors. For some, Research Methods is their first psychology course; others have had extensive coursework in the discipline. Many students have attended library instruction sessions in other non-psychology courses (specifically for English Composition) and see this session as an unnecessary repeat.

COOKING TIME

Cooking time is 60 minutes and serves fifteen to thirty students.

ACRL INFORMATION DIETARY STANDARDS ADDRESSED

Standard One: 1.1, 1.3, 1.4
Standard Two: 2.2, 2.3, 2.4, 2.5

MAIN COOKING TECHNIQUE

Peer-teaching, mini-demonstration, student-directed instruction

MAIN INGREDIENTS

- Computer access for all students
- Instructor's station
- Optional but recommended: Classroom management software such as Synchroneyes (to display students' computer screens to the entire class)

PREPARATION

Students should have their research proposal topics selected before the start of the class.

THE INSTRUCTION SESSION

1. Either the librarian or course instructor should review the concept of the literature review with the students (i.e. What is the purpose of the literature review? How is it structured? What is included?).

2. Take a quick survey of the class: How many students have been to a library instruction session before? What class were you attending? Who has used the PsycINFO database before?

3. Ask students who have used PsycINFO and/or been to a library instruction before to serve as experts for the class session. Tell them you will ask for their help and expertise later in the class.

4. Introduce the PsycINFO database and its basic interface.

5. Ask a student to volunteer his/her research proposal topic to use as a search example.

6. Ask the student experts to share searching tips and techniques on the following topics with their classmates:
   - keyword selection and combination
   - search limits
   - interpreting search results
   - narrowing search results
   - accessing the full-text of an article and storing it for future reading

7. Students can come up to the instructor station to teach their classmates, or if they are too shy to do that, they can also demonstrate from their own computer station and have it projected onto the classroom screen using classroom management software. Students can also direct the instructor's actions.

8. Ask the student experts if there is any other information they've learned from experience that they would like to share with their classmates.

9. Open the floor to questions from students to be directed to the student experts, with the librarian chiming in when needed.

ALLERGY WARNINGS

Many of our experts are students who have attended library instruction sessions before or used PsycINFO effectively and are therefore predisposed to view another library instruction session as boring, unhelpful repetition. Some may be a bit shy and reluctant to share information with their classmates.

You may have to draw them out a bit.

CHEF'S NOTE

There is no instructional situation I dislike more than the traditional database demonstration. I stand at the front of the classroom, enthusiastically offering effective searching tips, mouse-clicking my way through abstracts and subject terms, only to turn to my students and see rows of blank, empty stares. "Does anyone have any questions?" I ask. The response: Silence. Have they learned anything? Did I just bore them into a zombie-like state? It didn't take too many repeats of this scenario for me to wonder if perhaps there was a better way to teach students to use databases. This activity was born out of my frustration with point-and-click database demonstrations and my desire to make my students take a more active role in the learning process.

I'm always pleasantly surprised by how quickly students open up when you place them in the position of Expert Researcher. They are usually very eager to share their knowledge with their classmates, and their classmates almost always follow along and ask questions. This type of peer-teaching also makes the expert students (and as a consequence, their classmates) more willing to open up and ask questions about what they don't know. It provides a great opportunity for the librarian to step in with even more database knowledge. Best of all, this classroom technique avoids the yawn-inducing database demo. It breaks up the traditional show-and-tell into an interactive classroom experience.

Pineapple Upside-Down Cake:
Deconstructed Literature Review with Small Groups

In this recipe, a group of upper-level students work together to create a literature review of five articles.

Yvonne Nalani Meulemans, California State University at San Marcos, ymeulema@csusm.edu

NUTRITION INFORMATION
Students often assume that a literature review is merely a summary of a topic. The value in this recipe is that it demonstrates to students that a key part of a literature review is the identification of gaps in knowledge and provides an elegant segue to begin discussion about how the literature review is attached to their hypotheses and the rest of their project.

COOKING TIME
Cooking time is 60-75 minutes and serves twenty-five juniors and seniors in a research methods course.

ACRL INFORMATION DIETARY STANDARDS ADDRESSED
Standard Three
Standard Four

MAIN COOKING TECHNIQUE
Small group work, peer presentations

MAIN INGREDIENTS
- Literature review chart. The chart is blank, but the topic section is completed.
- Printout of abstracts of at least five scholarly articles on the same general area of study from PsycINFO (for example, five articles on factors leading to graduation among first generation college students). Each abstract is assigned a letter (A-E)

PREPARATION
Print out the abstracts and citations from a database for five articles on a particular topic. On the classroom's whiteboard, draw the blank literature review chart.

THE INSTRUCTION SESSION
1. **Introduction**
   - The session begins with the librarian indicating that the focus of the session will not be on which databases to use and how to use them, but instead will focus on developing students' understanding of the nature of a scholarly literature review.
   - In order to do this, the librarian explains, the entire class will write a literature review over the course of the class session.

2. **Small group work**
   - Place students in small groups. Groups of four students have worked best.
   - Each group will get an abstract and the blank literature review chart. One method of keeping track of which group has what abstract is to assign letters to each abstract and therefore, letters to each group: Group A will all receive the A abstract, Group B will all receive the B abstract, etc.
   - Groups are instructed to each read their assigned abstract and, as a group, complete the blanks for their abstract on the chart and transcribe it onto the classroom's blank chart on the whiteboard.

3. **Group discussion**
   - Once the classroom chart is completed, provide a few minutes for students to review it.
   - Then, start the discussion by asking students to articulate the class' findings on the topic and the question at the bottom of the chart.

ALLERGY WARNINGS

Prep time can be significant if a librarian is not familiar with the field of study. The course instructor can be very helpful in identifying a topic that could be used. This activity is particularly helpful in smaller classes where students may perceive themselves to be experienced researchers and may be reticent about yet another session from a librarian.

CHEF'S NOTE

- One negative aspect of this session is that there isn't much time (if any) to discuss suggested databases and other information regarding gathering information.
- Often times in research methods courses, the particular topics students select are so varied that it can be quite difficult to provide instruction that can apply to all students. The shared issue among students in such classes is that they must all complete the same assignment; the literature review being a major portion.
- Students should be encouraged to follow-up with a librarian should they need help gathering information.

Literature Review Chart				
HD 497: Applied Research in Human Development				
	Among college students, are there factors/clues/indicators about who will experience or perpetrate violence in a heterosexual, romantic relationship?			
	What does this article investigate?	Population Sampled?	Findings	Other key terms?
A				
B				
C				
D				
E				

What are some gaps in this body of research? What are some populations/aspects/areas that you don't see represented?

Can I do the "Ghosts of Gettysburg" for My Paper?

This recipe introduces students to the vagaries of local and historical research. Get each group started by using readily available resources. Searching the typical databases, though, does not always work for those of us in small-town universities.

Doug Cook, D.Ed., Reference Librarian and Professor, Shippensburg University, Shippensburg, PA, dlcook@ship.edu

NUTRITION INFORMATION
Freshmen writing students are asked to do a group PowerPoint presentation and individual short papers on a Local Landmark—for example, a town history or a local park. In the past, students have researched Hersheypark, Gettysburg Battlefield, etc.

COOKING TIME
Cooking time is 60 minutes and serves twenty freshmen.

ACRL INFORMATION DIETARY STANDARDS ADDRESSED
Standard One: 1.2.
Standard Two: 2.1, 2.2, 2.3, 2.4.
Standard Three: 3.1.

MAIN COOKING TECHNIQUE
Mini-demonstration, small-group work in computer lab

MAIN INGREDIENTS
- Computer lab
- Blackboard/whiteboard

PREPARATION
Compile resources on each of the general topics students have chosen.

THE INSTRUCTION SESSION
1. **Introduction**—10 minutes
   - Ask each group to describe the specifics of their topic to the whole class.
   - Keep track of topics on the board.
2. **Mini-lecture**—10 minutes
   - Do a mini-lecture and discussion highlighting the following resource types and how to find them, particularly in regard to their research topics.
     i. Books, media
     ii. Newspapers
     iii. Travel magazines
     iv. Web resources
     v. Site visits
3. **Group Research**—30 minutes
   - Give students time to begin research and discussion in their groups. Circulate to answer questions and identify profitable resources and topics.
4. **Debriefing**—10 minutes

ALLERGY WARNINGS
Students have a hard time understanding that they need to use actual resources—books, Web sites, interviews, etc.—for this project.

CHEF'S NOTE
I enjoy facilitating this session because it uses a different approach to the obligatory freshmen writing assignment I am continually challenged by the unusual topics students latch on to. One young man became fixated with the Ghosts of Gettysburg. This is not particularly a scholarly subject but I didn't want to dampen his enthusiasm. We started with Google and found a Web site advertising Ghost Tours. There is a tremendous amount of Web traffic regarding this topic, including numerous photos and accounts from ghost hunters and paranormal sites. One of the tour guides has written a number of books about the ghosts. What seemed to one skeptical librarian to be a bizarre topic, turned out to be pretty exciting.

Thanks to Dr. Cathy Dibello, English Dept., Shippensburg U. for the original recipe.

How Did the Civil Rights Movement Prompt the Anti-War Movement during the Vietnam Era?

This recipe assists students to find primary digital resources regarding recent U.S. historical events.

Danelle Moon, San Jose State University, Danelle.Moon@sjsu.edu
Nyle Monday, San Jose State University, Nyle.Monday@sjsu.edu

NUTRITION INFORMATION
This recipe is intended to reinforce primary source information literacy skills in a history/political science general education course.

COOKING TIME
Cooking time is 75 minutes. Serves twenty students.

ACRL INFORMATION DIETARY STANDARDS ADDRESSED
Standard One: 1.2
Standard Three: 3.1
Standard Four: 2.1, 2.2, 2.3, 2.4

MAIN COOKING TECHNIQUE
Brief demonstration, small group work, peer technology leader, PowerPoint presentations

MAIN INGREDIENTS
- Computer lab
- PowerPoint
- Instruction guide
- Flash drive stick

PREPARATION
Produce a PowerPoint sample project and resource guide, including instructions for creating a PowerPoint presentation.

THE INSTRUCTION SESSION
1. **Introduction**—10 minutes.
   a. Brief overview.
   b. Demonstration of the PowerPoint example.
2. **Activity**—35 minutes.
   a. Instructions
      i. Each group will locate four primary sources, including photographs, newspaper articles, oral histories, and video footage drawn from library primary source databases, Google, etc. Images must be downloaded and linked to their source.
      ii. Each group will produce a PowerPoint presentation with five slides.
   b. Topics
      i. Group 1—Kent State Killings.
      ii. Group 2—Justice in Buses.
      iii. Group 3—Black Panther Movement.
      iv. Group 4—Brown v. Board of Education.
      v. Group 5—Montgomery Bus Boycotts.
3. **Group Presentations**—10 minutes.

ALLERGY WARNINGS
Students varied in the ability to use the technology to produce the required PowerPoint.

CHEFS' NOTE
We enjoyed organizing this course and working with the students to locate digital primary sources. Students were actively engaged in the research process and worked effectively together to produce a creative PowerPoint presentation in a very short period.

Based upon the student output and ensuing discussion, the students enjoyed the discovery and research process.

Discovering the Value of Reference Sources

This recipe uses a matrix worksheet to help small groups of students analyze and evaluate reference sources

Shireen Deboo, Faculty Librarian, South Seattle Community College, Seattle Washington, sdeboo@sccd.ctc.edu

NUTRITION INFORMATION

This recipe will familiarize students with the purpose, function and value of reference sources. It will help them distinguish reference sources from other types of information. It will guide them to reference sources as a starting point for research projects, and help students distinguish online reference tools from other types of online sources.

COOKING TIME

Cooking time is 60 minutes. Serves ten to thirty undergraduates.

ACRL INFORMATION DIETARY STANDARDS ADDRESSED

Standard Two
Standard Three

MAIN COOKING TECHNIQUE

Hands-on exercise, group work

MAIN INGREDIENTS

- Computer lab
- Selected online reference sources, either free or subscription-based
- An assortment of your library's print reference sources.
- Matrix worksheet for each student

PREPARATION

Select a few examples of online reference sources and a few print reference sources. Bring enough copies of the matrix worksheet for each student.

THE INSTRUCTION SESSION

1. **Introduction**
   a. Begin by asking students if they can give an example of a common reference source. Hopefully someone will mention a dictionary, or the *Encyclopedia Britannica*.
   b. Provide a definition of *reference work*. If the definition refers to a *book*, this is a good time to remind students that today, reference sources can be online or in print.
   c. Be sure to help students understand how a reference work is different from other types of sources. Illustrate how it provides an entry point, explains the basic vocabulary, and offers a quick overview on a particular topic or subject.
   d. Beyond providing and discussing the definition of a reference work, explain that at the college level, reference resources offer much

more than *World Book* or *Webster's Dictionary*. Introduce the idea of subject dictionaries and specialized encyclopedias, etc, by showing examples of each.

2. **Worksheet**—20 minutes
   a. Provide each student or team with a worksheet that assigns them to one online reference resource and one print reference source and includes a matrix of questions to answer about the sources.
   b. This worksheet will ask the students to engage with the resource, use it, and explore its features, its organization, and its content. It also asks the students to approach the resource from a critical perspective and provide feedback about usability, target audience, and overall quality.

3. **Report back to class**
   a. Students complete the worksheet and then share their findings in short report outs to the class.

ALLERGY WARNINGS

Students may be confused or frustrated by the matrix questions about publication frequency or authors if that data is not easily found in their sources.

CHEF'S NOTE

By asking students for both descriptive and critical feedback, we are teaching students that reference sources, like any other sources, can be imperfect. They can be imperfect in content, breadth, depth, presentation or organization. Having them discover these imperfections can be a teaching moment.

We can also remind them that a reference source might be perfectly useful for a few types of information needs, but not appropriate for other needs.

Reference Sources Matrix		
Select one print reference source and one online reference source. You can use any online reference source accessed from a library website.		
	Print Reference Source	Online Reference Source
Cite sources in MLA style.		
Give two examples of questions that could be answered using this reference source.		
How frequently is this source published?		
Does this source have one author or several authors and one editor?		
Who do you think is the targeted audience for this source?		
Describe how this source is organized. Is there an index, a table of contents, a guide to using the source?		
Provide an analysis of this source: is it easy to use or difficult? Is the layout useful, or how could it be better? What is missing?		

6. DISCIPLINE RELATED RESEARCH

The Art of Database Searching

This recipe encourages art students to represent search strategies and hints in a visual format.

Dawn Eckenrode, Reference and Instruction Librarian, SUNY Fredonia, Fredonia, NY, dawn.eckenrode@fredonia.edu

NUTRITION INFORMATION

This recipe is intended for students in a freshman, introductory art class. It is designed to introduce students to a variety of tools appropriate for researching art topics, as well as to basic database searching techniques. In addition to providing an introduction to the discipline, the goals of the course include building a sense of community among the students.

COOKING TIME

Cooking time is 80 minutes and serves up to fifty freshmen.

ACRL INFORMATION DIETARY STANDARDS ADDRESSED

Standard Two: 2.2, 2.3
Standard Four: 4.1, 4.3

MAIN COOKING TECHNIQUE

Hands-on exercises, small-group work, discussion and reflection, presentation (visual, kinesthetic, and auditory elements)

MAIN INGREDIENTS

- Computer access for all students
- Room for students to work in groups
- Instructor's station
- Poster board for each group
- Markers, crayons, glitter glue, etc.
- Goofy prizes, such as twirly straws, whoopee cushions, and silly putty are popular.

PREPARATION

Handouts and materials such as prizes and art supplies will need to be gathered.

THE INSTRUCTION SESSION

1. **Introduction**
   a. Explain purpose of the class.

2. **Group activity 1**
   a. Each group is assigned a different library database in which they must conduct a pre-determined search.
   b. A worksheet is provided to guide the students through the steps in the search, directing them to use the various features and functions of the databases, as well as selected search techniques.
   c. The instructor acts as facilitator during this exercise.

3. **Group activity 2**
   a. Once the groups complete the pre-determined searches, they are directed to complete a search on an art topic they are interested in learning more about.
   b. Based on their searching, the students answer the following questions:
      i. What search terms did you use?
      ii. How many hits did you retrieve? Were your results relevant to the topic?
      iii. What features did you find useful when using this database?

4. **Report back**
   a. The groups of students are asked to share problems or difficulties.
   b. While the students share their observations, the librarian facilitates discussion, answers questions, conducts demonstrations, and makes elaborations, wherever appropriate.

5. **Poster activity**—30 minutes

ALLERGY WARNINGS

This class can get a little chaotic, so it helps immensely if the students' professor is someone who will actively participate in facilitating the group work. It is also important to provide the students with adequate time to work on their posters and present what they have learned.

CHEF'S NOTE

This is a fun and active lesson for both the students and the librarian. I'm always impressed by the level of thought the students put into explaining the concepts learned, such as developing and articulating an understanding of research as an iterative process. The students appreciate the creative component, and I always enjoy their quirky drawings of WorldCat (picture the earth with whiskers, ears, and a tail) and of me, the helpful librarian.

Special thanks to Dr. Leesa Rittelmann, Department of Visual Arts and New Media at SUNY Fredonia, and her ART 100 students.

a. The groups of students are then given a piece of poster board and colored markers. They are asked to draw a visual representation of three things learned in class.
b. The groups of students present their posters and the concepts learned.
c. Students vote on the best poster and prizes are awarded.

"I Just Need One More Piece of Business Information!"

Business students learn firsthand that library databases are valuable by working together as a group to search for information on a particular company.

Aaron W. Dobbs, Systems and Electronic Resources/Web Librarian and Assistant Professor, Shippensburg University of Pennsylvania, awdobbs@ship.edu

NUTRITION INFORMATION
This recipe is intended for students who need to present a comprehensive overview of a company for a class assignment. Students work in groups to compare free Web resources with library business resources. They should already have received a decent overview of library resources in a previous session.

COOKING TIME
Cooking time is 75 minutes. Serves forty introductory-level business students.

ACRL INFORMATION DIETARY STANDARDS ADDRESSED
Standard One: 1.1
Standard Two: 2.1, 2.2, 2.3
Standard Three: 3.1, 3.3
Standard Four: 4.1, 4.2, 4.3

MAIN COOKING TECHNIQUE
Short demonstration, small-group work, peer assistance, presentations, jigsaw

MAIN INGREDIENTS
- Web access and PowerPoint for all students
- Handouts

PREPARATION
This session requires coordination of the classroom assignment with a business professor plus the librarian's strong familiarity with available business resources, including free Web, subscription databases, and paper sources. An outline of expected strengths and weaknesses of each resource, for comparison with students' discoveries, will aid in the evaluation and reinforcement of students' understanding of business resources.

THE INSTRUCTION SESSION
1. **Introduction**—10 minutes
   a. Review class assignment with students.
   b. Remind them that they have had library research experience in the past.
   c. Reintroduce related free Web, library subscription, and paper resources
   d. Briefly demonstrate any complex interfaces
   e. Describe the in-class competition
      i. There are three questions that will be handed out, one question per row, two teams per row. One team per question will use publicly available (free) internet sources, the other will use the library databases described.
      ii. Hand out project descriptions to each group

2. **Group Activity**—30 minutes
   a. Groups work on answering questions with assigned resources
   b. Groups for the two teams for each question collaborate on providing a short summary file and presentation about perceived strengths and weaknesses of recommended and not recommended resources and reasoning on how this was determined and why to use of avoid each tool
   c. Each row will produce a PowerPoint presentation, not less than six slides (including a title slide with group members listed), supporting their standpoint.
   d. Present this exercise as a contest to see which group is the most cogent and helpful.

3. **Report back group**—20 minutes

a. Collect presentations for display from instructor's machine.
b. Groups present their findings.
c. Encourage professor to post summary files/presentations on course management system

ALLERGY WARNINGS

Occasionally students or entire sections will not quite understand what is asked of them, since this session is more free-form than many similar sessions. When this occurs it is easier and more class-efficient to take these student(s) aside for explanations; when re-explaining to an entire class, often the re-explanation confuses other students more than clarifies for the original student(s).

CHEF'S NOTE

There are many free resources that are available on the internet that provide some information on companies and industries. While learning about library databases, students need to understand that these databases provide more information than the free databases.

There is usually one PowerPoint guru in each group. Seek that person out at the beginning of the session, and make them mandatory presentation creator. However, all students must assist in research.

Questions for groups:

1. Find and share the company financials of a local business (offer three or four as options).
    a. *Row 1, Group 1*—Library resources: Moody's, ABI/Inform, ValueLine, etc.
    b. *Row 1, Group 2*—Free sources: Yahoo or Google Finance, FreeEdgar, Wall Street Journal, etc.

2. Find a company's major competitors and industry rating/market share.
    a. *Row 2, Group 1*—Library resources: ABI/Inform, EconLit, Business Source Premier, etc.
    b. *Row 2, Group 2*—Free Resources: Yahoo or Google Finance, FreeEdgar, New York Times, etc.

3. Perform a very brief industry SWOT analysis listing the major SWOTs for a given industry.
    a. *Row 3, Group 1*—Library resources: ABI/Inform, Business Source Premier, Sage, Emerald, etc.
    b. *Row 3, Group 2*—Free Resources: Yahoo or Google Finance, FreeEdgar, New York Times, etc.

MeSHed Potatoes and Gravy

MeShed Potatoes and Gravy uses group discussion and guided research to whip up the starchy controlled vocabulary, MeSH—Medical Subject Headings.

Alice L. Daugherty, Louisiana State University, adaugher@lsu.edu; Michael F. Russo, Louisiana State University, Mrusso1@lsu.edu

NUTRITION INFORMATION

This recipe is useful for students in the Communication Sciences and Disorders program. The class has to prepare a literature review on a topic within the hearing sciences. The students are proficient researchers, already familiar with the EBSCO interface and Boolean operators. Prior to arriving at class, students are asked to have their topics in mind.

COOKING TIME

Cooking time is approximately 60 minutes and serves no more than fifteen seniors.

ACRL INFORMATION DIETARY STANDARDS ADDRESSED

Standard One: 1.1, 1.2
Standard Two: 2.2, 2.3, 2.4, 2.5
Standard Three: 3.1, 3.2
Standard Four: 4.1
Standard Five: 5.3

MAIN COOKING TECHNIQUE

Lecture, demonstration, group practice, independent practice

MAIN INGREDIENTS

- Computers with Internet access for students
- Teacher workstation
- Laser pointer
- A pinch of interest

PREPARATION

The preparation for this lesson consists of gathering appropriate discipline-specific examples in order for the demonstration to run smoothly. Prepare to present MeSH terms illustrating the Major Concept or the Explode feature, as well as the related subheadings and cross references. Such terms may include Auditory Perceptual Disorders, Cochlear Implants, Psychoacoustics, Tinnitus, and a variety of other audiological terms.

THE INSTRUCTION SESSION

1. **Introduction**
   a. Instructor provides a brief introduction to the importance of using MEDLINE as a database for the hearing sciences.
   b. Instructor points out the EBSCO interface and the functions available (saving to drive, e-mailing, saving to folders, saving to My EBSCOhost, finding full text through the link resolver, etc.)
   c. Instructor explains and demonstrates controlled vocabulary MeSH using the example term *Tinnitus* as a Major Concept.

2. **Group research**
   a. At this time the instructor selects one of the student's topics and the class as a whole works together with the instructor to narrow and focus search results using MeSH terms.

3. **Individual research**
   a. The students then work independently using MeSH and locating articles specific to their literature review topics. The instructor walks around to each individual to make sure the students are on task.
   b. The students e-mail a full-text article to their professor of record and also to their own e-mail account.

ALLERGY WARNINGS

Many of the students involved in this instruction had already completed a library instruction course. However, even with that knowledge base, the students needed further instruction about databases. They did not seem to understand that one vendor (EBSCO) could have several databases of different discipline content.

The students did seem to grasp the concept of controlled vocabulary. The instructor compared controlled vocabulary to pop-culture items such as tagging and folksonomies.

The students asked several questions about how to export citations into the citation management system Endnote.

CHEFS' NOTE

This small class worked very well together. Even when they were working independently the students would discuss their findings and refine their searches based on the dialogue with their classmates.

A handout listing other periodical indexes and databases, core journals, and Library of Congress call numbers for speech and hearing was provided.

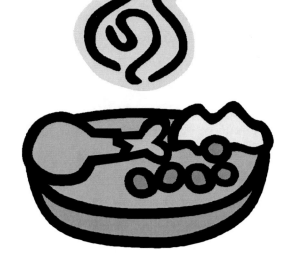

Garnishing Literacy Instruction with Google

Google provides search scaffolding to help classroom teachers to learn to better search ERIC.

Cynthia Crosser, Social Science and Humanities Reference Librarian, University of Maine, Orono, ME, cynthia.crosser@umit.maine.edu

NUTRITION INFORMATION

This recipe is designed as a database demonstration of ERIC using the EBSCO interface, as students prepare to write their first research paper in the M.Ed. program in Literacy. The purpose is to ease teachers into the research process by beginning with the knowledge they already have about Google.

COOKING TIME

Cooking time is 60 minutes and serves 20 graduate students.

ACRL INFORMATION DIETARY STANDARDS ADDRESSED

Standard Two: 2.1, 2.2, 2.3
Standard Four: 4.1, 4.2

MAIN COOKING TECHNIQUE

Hands-on group, individual work

MAIN INGREDIENTS

- Computer access for all students
- Instructor's station
- Handout

PREPARATION

This session works best when you collaborate with the faculty member. It is important to know in advance at least some of the topics that students will be working on and to practice searching before the session. It is assumed that the librarian is familiar with the subject area.

THE INSTRUCTION SESSION

Part One—Handout on similarities and differences between Google and ERIC.

Using Google demonstrate searching relevant topics on the Web.

Part Two—Instructor Demonstration

Use a relevant topic to demonstrate searching ERIC. If you have not been provided with an example topic in advance, then use a topic relevant to the subject. Make sure that you do NOT choose the very best search terms. Tell them what you are thinking while you do the search. When you get the results, make changes to better search terms based on the results (e.g., database descriptors, terms to narrow/broaden search).

Part Three—Interactive Class Search

Ask for volunteers to provide a topic and search terms to locate relevant resources. Everyone in the class searches together. This needs to be very interactive. Encourage students to discuss changing search terms based on results.

Part Four—Individual Searching

Let students conduct their own searches. Be ready to offer individual help when needed. Let students e-mail, print, or save full text articles and citations for articles without full text copy.

ALLERGY WARNINGS
This is not a recipe for extensive search of research literature for an advanced seminar.

CHEF'S NOTE
This training does more than just provide knowledge for conducting research. It frequently leads to requests for more research assistance. Even if students don't need more help for this project, they will feel comfortable contacting you for future research needs.

Handout on similarities and differences between Google and ERIC

1. Google automatically stems in the search process. EBSCO databases require the use of the wildcard * to stem in the search process.

   Example: In Google, **child** will search for both *child* and *children*. In ERIC: **child*** will search for both *child* and *children*.

2. Google automatically uses proximity with AND in the search process. ERIC automatically uses only proximity in the search process. In ERIC, you need to put AND between terms in the same search box unless the terms are highly likely to occur next to each other. You can use AND in Google but it is not necessary.

   Examples: In Google **reading fluency** will search first for the phrase *reading fluency* and then for both terms separately. In ERIC **reading fluency** will search for the phrase. In both Google and ERIC **reading AND ESL** will search for both terms separately.

3. Google degrades in the search process. If you enter five terms and Google can only match four, you get the best results for the four terms. If you enter five terms using ERIC and it can only match four, then you don't get any results.

   Example: In Google **reading AND ESL AND phonology AND fluency AND middle school** produces results. In ERIC this search will not produce results.

Whipping up the "Why" Paper: Inquiry into Diverse Perspectives

Students are introduced to various databases that provide access to alternative perspectives and to an advanced organizer designed to foster critical evaluation of sources.

Jennifer Fabbi, Head of the Curriculum Materials Library and Special Assistant to the Dean, University of Nevada, Las Vegas Libraries, jennifer.fabbi@unlv.edu; Paula McMillen, Education Librarian, University of Nevada, Las Vegas Libraries, paula. mcmillen@unlv.edu; Abigail Hawkins, Instructional Designer, abbyhawkins7@gmail.com

NUTRITION INFORMATION

In a Valuing Cultural Diversity course, required for all undergraduate education majors, students are asked to write a "Why" paper to investigate and understand alternative perspectives, looking particularly at the perspectives of a cultural group different from their own (Sleeter, Torres, & Laughlin, 2004).

Sleeter, C., M.N.Torres, and P. Laughlin. 2004. Scaffolding Conscientization through Inquiry in Teacher Education. Teacher Education Quarterly 31 (1):81-96.

COOKING TIME

Cooking time is at least 60 minutes.

ACRL INFORMATION DIETARY STANDARDS ADDRESSED

Standard Three: 3.1, 3.2, 3.4, 3.5, 3.6
Standard One: 1.1, 1.2, 1.3
Standard Two: 2.1, 2.2, 2.3, 2.4, 2.5
Standard Four: 4.1

MAIN COOKING TECHNIQUE

Individual and small-group work, large-group discussion, instructor demonstration, hands-on interactions with information sources

MAIN INGREDIENTS

- Computer access for all students
- Instructor's station with projector
- Access to the internet and appropriate subscription databases (education research as well as gender- or culture-focused sources, e.g., ERIC, Ethnic Newswatch, etc.)
- Whiteboard /blackboard

PREPARATION

Students will have identified a "Why" question, developed a concept map based on this question, and pre-approved both with their primary instructor. In constructing the concept map, students will have identified key terms, synonyms and related terms pertinent to their original "Why" question.

THE INSTRUCTION SESSION

1. **Introduction**—1 minute
   - Introduce self and purpose of instruction session.
2. **Insider/Outsider pairs**—5-7 minutes
   - Have students work in pairs to define and identify benefits of both insider and outsider perspectives.
   - Bring their ideas back to large group discussion.
3. **Primary vs. secondary sources**—10-12 minutes
   - Using a think-pair-share approach, have students write down examples of primary and secondary sources.
   - As a whole class, write students' examples on the board under two columns labeled Primary and Secondary Sources. Ask students to indicate which sources would likely be from an insider or outsider perspective. Note that the remainder of the session will have students explore places where they can find information that provides insider and/or outsider perspectives.

4. **Hands-on education research**—15 minutes
   - Introduce and hand out library assignment (Sources Table). Relate it to completing their "Why" Paper (i.e. identifying sources from insider and outsider perspectives).
   - Demonstrate a search in an education research database. Explain and show through your search strategies the connection between the concept map and keyword search.
   - Model evaluating one of the resources found; use the questions posed in the table and involve the class in completing one of the table rows.
   - Give students hands-on time to find a resource relevant to their own question in that database and have them complete a row in their own Sources Table.

5. **Hands-on culture or gender-focused research**—15 minutes
   - Repeat using a culture or gender-focused database. Indicate that an insider perspective is more likely found in these databases than in a general or education database.

6. **Individual research**
   - Provide handout with additional databases and Web sites.
   - Give students the remainder of the time to search their own topic with the librarian available for individual consultation.

ALLERGY WARNINGS

Students may not fully understand the distinction between primary and secondary sources.

Students narrowly evaluate sources based on their relevance to the subject matter of their topics. Particularly for this class and assignment, another criteria we want students to consider is the credibility and perspective of the source's author vis-à-vis the topic at hand. This needs to be emphasized during the in-class demonstration of evaluating sources found in the databases as well as criteria such as accuracy, scope, and currency.

CHEFS' NOTE

For many students, because this is their first encounter with emotionally-charged diversity topics, they are often more engaged with the project than is typical for lower division students.

See *Cooking Up Concept Maps* in Section 5 to learn to create a concept map.

Sources Table	
1. Source Location	
2. Source Type	
3. Voice/Perspective of Writer	
4. Insider (I) or Outsider (O)	
5. Citation Information (see APA guidelines for specific information needed for your source type)	
6. Why (or why not) is this source of information important to your question? Provide at least 2 reasons or pieces of evidence for your decision.	

Alphabet Soup: Using Children's Literature Databases to Plan Lessons on Letters of the Alphabet

Your students will choose a letter of the alphabet, find a children's book related to that letter, and write a brief lesson plan using the book.

Kelly Heider, D.Ed., Education Librarian, Assistant Professor, Indiana University of PA, kheider@iup.edu

NUTRITION INFORMATION

This recipe is intended for undergraduate Early Childhood Education Majors. Students will learn how to use children's literature databases to choose appropriate books for classroom instruction.

COOKING TIME

Cooking time for this recipe is 75 minutes. Serves twenty-six education students, ideally.

ACRL INFORMATION DIETARY STANDARDS ADDRESSED

Standard One: 1.1, 1.2, 1.3, 1.4.
Standard Two: 2.1, 2.2, 2.3, 2.4, 2.5.
Standard Three: 3.1, 3.2, 3.3, 3.4, 3.5, 3.6, 3.7.
Standard Four: 4.1, 4.2, 4.3.
Standard Five: 5.1, 5.2, 5.3.

MAIN COOKING TECHNIQUE

Discovery Learning

MAIN INGREDIENTS

- Instructor's computer with LCD projector
- Enough computers for each student in the class
- Large soup pot and ladle
- Stencil-cut letters of the alphabet
- Lesson plan template handout
- Cat puppet (optional)

PREPARATION

Using stencils, trace and cut letters of the alphabet out of card stock. Copy lesson plan template handouts for students. Prepare for *Bad Kitty* book talk. (*Bad Kitty* is the story of a cat that behaves badly when it finds out there isn't any food in the house.)

THE INSTRUCTION SESSION

1. **Introduction**
   - Read *Bad Kitty* by Nick Bruel (New Milford, Conn: Roaring Brook Press, 2005) and drop stencil-cut letters into the soup pot as you come to each letter in the story.
   - If using a cat puppet, allow the puppet to add the letters and stir the soup with the ladle.

Photograph by Doug Shumar, artist/illustrator, Indiana University of PA, dashumar@iup.edu

2. **Teacher Talk**
   - Students will locate two children's literature databases (i.e. Children's Literature Comprehensive Database and NoveList K-8) on the library Web site.

- Students will learn how to search for books on letters of the alphabet by watching a brief demonstration.
- After the demonstration, students will receive the lesson plan template and choose letters from the soup pot.

3. **Discovery learning and guided practice**
   - Using the children's literature databases, each student will find a book that teaches his/her letter. (Discovery learning and guided practice occur here, since students will discover features of the database, such as book reviews, reading levels, author links, book talks, curriculum connections, etc., and ask the librarian questions when they don't understand or need clarification.)
   - When each student has settled on a book, he/she will write the title and author on his/her stencil-cut letter and design a lesson plan that incorporates the book using the lesson plan template handout.
   - Students will drop their stencil-cut letters (with the title and author of a children's book written on them) into the soup pot when they have completed their lesson plans.

4. **Assessment**
   - The librarian will randomly choose letters from the soup pot and ask the students to give brief summaries of their lesson plans to the class.
   - Students will be asked to stress which database features were most helpful to them as they designed their lessons.

ALLERGY WARNINGS

Before presenting this lesson to early childhood education majors, make sure that students have already had some experience writing lesson plans. Design the lesson plan template handout to meet the lesson plan guidelines set forth by your university's college of education.

CHEF'S NOTE

Follow-up Librarian Activity: The librarian could use the students' stencil-cut letters to create a list of alphabet books or even a booklet of alphabet lesson plans to distribute to the class for future use.

Sample Lesson Plan Format:

1. HEADING
2. RATIONALE AND BACKGROUND
3. LESSON OBJECTIVES
4. LIST OF MATERIALS/RESOURCES
5. PROCEDURES
   a) Introduction and Motivation
   b) Lesson Body
   c) Lesson Closure
6. EVALUATION
   a) Student Assessment
   b) Self-Evaluation

Lesson Plan Template

I chose the following book to incorporate into my lesson on the letter _____. (Please cite the book in APA Style below.)

I used the following children's literature database(s) to find my book and plan my lesson:
_____ Children's Literature Comprehensive Database
_____ NoveList K-8

The feature(s) in this/these database(s) that was/were most helpful to me:

My lesson plan follows:

Now I Know My ABC's (of Children's Literature)

Students use an alphabetized list of subject headings to become familiar with a children's literature collection.

Sara Holder, Liaison Librarian, Education Library and Curriculum Resources Centre, McGill University, Montréal, Quebec, sara.holder@mcgill.ca

NUTRITION INFORMATION

This recipe provides education students with practice searching the library catalog, and specifically, searching for children's literature for which subject headings are usually not very detailed. It also acquaints students with the physical arrangement of the children's literature collection, which is for the most part, based on author name rather than subject.

COOKING TIME

Cooking time is 1 hour. Recipe serves a maximum of thirty undergraduate education majors.

ACRL INFORMATION DIETARY STANDARDS ADDRESSED

Standard Two: 2.2, 2.3, 2.4
Standard Four: 4.2, 4.3

MAIN COOKING TECHNIQUE

Demonstration, hands-on group work, peer assistance

MAIN INGREDIENTS

- Computer access for students
- Instructor's station
- Access to a printer (preferable but not absolutely necessary)
- Subject list handouts (or link to online copies).

PREPARATION

You will need some time to compile the subject list handouts. Time needed for this will vary depending on how many subject options you offer

THE INSTRUCTION SESSION

1. **Introduction**—10 minutes
   - Give a brief overview of what type of information can be found in a library catalog record and how to narrow a search to the children's literature collection.
   - Explain the arrangement of the literature collection and how it differs from other collections.

2. **Searching the catalog**
   - Break class into groups of two or three (depending on class size).
   - Distribute subject list handouts or direct students to the location of online copies.
   - Assign each group a set of three letters of the alphabet.
   - Each group will choose one subject from the lists for each of their letters and search the catalog to compile a list of three books on each of their subjects (to avoid duplication among groups). Each group will assign one of its members to take notes on the search strategies used.
   - Circulate among the groups offering help and encouragement.

3. **Retrieving books from the collection**
   - If you have access to a printer, ask each group to print their list and show it to you before going into the stacks to find their books. If there is no printer, ask to see their list on the computer and instruct them to copy down the call numbers on scrap paper to take with them to the stacks.
   - Each group should bring back three books, preferably one on each of their three subjects.

4. **Discussion of strategies**
   - Ask each group to present their books and explain (briefly) the strategies they used to find them.

ALLERGY WARNINGS

- The more subjects you can compile, the better. In the larger classes where several groups may have the same letters assigned, they all seem to choose the same subjects. I have made up several different A-Z lists that I distribute. This ensures that in large sessions where letter assignments are duplicated, each group has a different list of subjects.
- Alert your shelving staff in advance of presenting this activity as there will be up to ninety books to re-shelve!

CHEF'S NOTE

This may seem like an overly simple activity but it helps tremendously with students' understanding of how the library catalog works. I find that subject searching in the catalog is a common stumbling block and something with which students are hesitant to ask for help. This activity is fun and the knowledge seems to stick, making the participants into more confident, effective searchers.

Utilizing (Bridge) Failure to Ensure Information Literacy Success

Busted bridges bring bright students into contact with searching in the Engineering literature.

Eric Resnis, Instruction Coordinator, Miami University Libraries, Oxford OH, eric.resnis@muohio.edu

NUTRITION INFORMATION

This recipe utilizes YouTube videos of bridge collapses to help students begin research for a bridge failure and truss design assignment. The activity reacquaints students with the research process, while providing an introduction to the Engineering literature. Students will have had a library resources overview in a previous session.

COOKING TIME

Cooking time is 90 minutes and serves twenty-five second-semester freshmen.

acrl INFORMATION DIETARY STANDARDS
ADDRESSED
Standard One: 1.2, 1.4
Standard Two: 2.1, 2.2, 2.3, 2.4

MAIN COOKING TECHNIQUE

Mini-demonstration, group work, peer assistance, discussion

MAIN INGREDIENTS

- Workstations for 25 students with group work space
- Optional: Teacher Software (NetOp School or similar)
- Optional: Microsoft PowerPoint and Clickers (also called Teacher Response System)

PREPARATION

Not a great deal of preparation is required, although the instructor should have a working knowledge of common bridge failures and bridge truss types. Students will be encouraged to view a basic online tutorial before the session to refresh their knowledge of library resources—http://me.lib.muohio.edu/eas102.

THE INSTRUCTION SESSION

1. **Introduction**—10 minutes
   a. Go over the assignment.
   b. Give a brief review/lecture of locations for finding Engineering literature (including Google/search engines, library catalog, basic Engineering databases).
   c. During the lecture, use Clickers to gauge student familiarity with each resource mentioned.

2. **Group research**—20 minutes
   a. At the end of the lecture, utilize Clicker data to assign groups (if you don't have Clickers, simply ask for volunteers). There will be a total of six groups—two groups for each resource (with four to five people in each). Each group will have a leader who is familiar with the resource and will lead in teaching the others in the group.
   b. Students utilize YouTube to find a video of a bridge collapse, and then use their library resource to find more information about that bridge collapse (including the reason for failure)
3. **Report back**—30 minutes
   a. At the end of the 20 minutes, class reconvenes. Each group has 3-5 minutes to present their findings, including a snippet from the YouTube seedling video. Each group will be given control over classroom computers using the Teacher Software. After each presentation, a brief discussion will ensue to reinforce what the group found and its place in the research process.

ALLERGY WARNINGS

- Students may complain about their group placement, but generally will complete satisfactory work.
- Knowing about bridge collapse and bridge trusses is essential to being an effective facilitator of the discussion.

CHEF'S NOTE

- This session is vastly different from talking head presentations.
- While they are encouraged to view a refresher tutorial before class, I always expect that only a few of them actually look. Many students say afterwards that looking at the tutorial would have made their group work much easier (and many students use it during their group work).
- This session has generally been well received as it gives the students an opportunity to engage in research, with me playing guide/facilitator instead of strictly teacher. Although the group work is not competitive, students enjoy utilizing the Teacher Software to control all the computers.
- I also provided a handout with a recap of techniques and librarian contact information.

Undergraduate English Potpourri: Peer Teaching of Periodical Indexes
This entrée is peer teaching about periodical indexes with a bit of "candy as bribery" thrown in for good measure.

Robin Bergart, Academic Liaison Librarian, University of Guelph, Ontario, Canada, rbergart@uoguelph.ca

NUTRITION INFORMATION
Groups of students use a list of guiding questions to examine and present a periodical database to the rest of the class. As we know, the best way to learn is to teach. This session provides a full sensory experience of sight, sound, touch, taste, and smell. Like the potpourri we made in grade school by sticking cloves into oranges, this class is easy for the librarian instructor to put together and it smells great!

COOKING TIME
Cooking time is 75-90 minutes. Serves twenty junior or senior level English Literature students.

ACRL INFORMATION DIETARY STANDARDS ADDRESSED
Standard One: 1.2
Standard Two: 2.2

MAIN COOKING TECHNIQUE
Small group work; peer teaching, jigsaw method

MAIN INGREDIENTS
- A heap of print periodicals from the literature section of your library
- Handout
- Individually-wrapped chocolate or candy

PREPARATION
Little advance preparation is required other than to whip up a copy of the students' course syllabus, review the key periodical indexes relevant to the course, and create a simple handout of guided questions.

THE INSTRUCTION SESSION
1. **Periodicals Palate Cleanser**—10 minutes
   a. Before students enter the room, place a candy on each keyboard
   b. Check the students' understanding of what periodicals and periodical indexes are and what they're good for. Use the pile of print periodicals for dramatic effect to demonstrate how time-consuming it would be to search through each one individually.
   c. Introduce the periodical indexes to be examined and present the next activity.
2. **Main Course**—50 minutes
   a. **Group Research**—15 minutes
      i. This is the meat of the session. Students work in small groups to learn the ins and outs of a particular periodical index and then teach that index to the whole class.
      ii. Assign one periodical index to each group and provide guiding questions handout to help them prepare their presentations.

iii. Each group must prepare a short lesson about the use and value of their assigned periodical index, which they will subsequently present to the rest of the class.

iv. Walk around. You can see if students are having problems, and you will get some exercise!

b. Group presentations—35 minutes.

i. Using the instructor's computer and screen

ii. Provide a little time at the end to prompt reflection on what they had difficulty with and what they learned.

3. Dessert—0 minutes. Dessert was already served. Nice try!

ALLERGY WARNINGS
Students aren't always attentive when their peers are teaching, so keep things moving along and help to facilitate interactions between the peer teachers and the peer students.

GUIDING QUESTIONS

1. How do you find this periodical index on the library website?
2. Demonstrate how to find an article on a topic related to your course.
3. Demonstrate how to find more articles on the same topic using descriptors/ subject terms.
4. Do a similar search in Google Scholar and compare your results.
5. Demonstrate how to get full text articles from your periodical index.
6. Demonstrate how to export a citation to RefWorks.

CHEF'S NOTE
I included the MLA International Bibliography, Humanities Index, JSTOR, and Project Muse in this exercise. You can ask each group to do the same search in each database so they can see the different search results you get with different databases.

Try if you can to fit the candy with your particular class theme, e.g. for a class on British Literature use English toffee or Quality Street chocolate; for a class on science fiction use rocket candy. While some may see this as bribery, providing sugar to students sits on firm pedagogical footing. It awakens the taste buds and olfactory channels (two sadly under-utilized senses in most library instruction classes). It induces a mental state of curiosity and wonder (what is this piece of candy doing on my computer!?). And if done right, it creates a rich environment whereby the candy in question contributes to and amplifies the theme of the particular English Literature class.

Digging for Information Artifacts

Common terms used to describe historical occurrences often do not come into use until after the event. Searching for first hand accounts of these events takes keyword brainstorming.

Melissa Becher, American University, mbecher@american.edu

NUTRITION INFORMATION

This appetizer is useful when students have an assignment that takes them on a collision course with historical sources—especially when controlled vocabulary is limited or nonexistent. It helps students get out of their twenty-first century mind-set when coming up with historical search terms. To facilitate this, students are asked to search for terms that have historical baggage.

COOKING TIME

Cooking time is 20 minutes. Serves twenty-five freshmen or sophomores.

ACRL INFORMATION DIETARY STANDARDS ADDRESSED

Standard 2
Standard 3

MAIN COOKING TECHNIQUE

Hands-on searching combined with brainstorming

MAIN INGREDIENTS

- Computer Access for all students
- Historical Newspaper Database (I use the Washington Post—Historical, but others may be substituted)
- Whiteboard

PREPARATION

Test the searches in your newspaper database to make sure they work to your satisfaction. Other searches can be used as long as the first one is about a phenomenon with various historical names and the other search is one that gives better results when linked to a proper noun.

THE INSTRUCTION SESSION

1. **Introduction**—Words change over time and people of different times have called things by different names. Newspapers are historical artifacts as well as information sources in that they reflect their times. If you think as a person of the time, you'll have better luck in finding information from these sources.

2. **First example—post traumatic stress disorder**
   - Have students do a search on post traumatic stress disorder and ask them for the year of the earliest article they can find. It will likely be 1980 or later.
   - Ask the students "So, we didn't have this phenomenon before 1980? What about all those other wars of the past? Possibly it was called something different."
   - Brainstorm more historical terms that describe post traumatic stress disorder. Write student suggestions on the whiteboard, e.g., shell shock or battle fatigue. Have the students search those terms. The results should be

significantly higher. Shell shock is vintage WWI, and battle fatigue comes into use around WWII.

- Explain that the reason the students cannot put in post traumatic stress disorder and get all the results in the database is that most newspaper databases do not have subject headings. Subject headings help us immensely by collecting all variant historical terms under one modern word, so that we can find things more easily. One strategy in dealing with a database that has no subject headings is to link a search to a proper noun, either a person or place name. The next search will demonstrate that concept.

3. **Second example—holocaust**
- Have students limit their next search to 1943-1946. Ask them to search the term holocaust.
- What will come up are links to articles about hotel fires and the like. Explain that this is because holocaust is a term that came into common use later to describe the horror of Nazi genocide. Ask the students to think of proper nouns associated with what we now think of as the Holocaust. Names of concentration camps, names of Nazi officials, Jews, Nazis, etc. should work. Write these on the whiteboard.

- Have the students search some of these terms. They should find much more relevant material.

ALLERGY WARNINGS
Be prepared to handle any question about historical slurs for ethnic or other minority groups. I've only had this come up once—my answer was reiterating that newspapers are historical artifacts and they reflect the mainstream views of their time, not our time.

CHEF'S NOTE
I always tell students, "This is going to blow your mind." They smirk, but when I ask later, "Now didn't that blow your mind"? Some of them actually say, "Yes."

Students like looking at the scanned newspaper articles, so I've found that building in a couple of minutes of look time does no harm.

Fact Check au jus

This recipe challenges students with a real-life example from the global warming debate. Students watch a video clip and attempt to verify the truth of a statement.

Michael F. Russo, Louisiana State University, Mrusso1@lsu.edu; Alice L. Daugherty, Louisiana State University, adaugher@lsu.edu

NUTRITION INFORMATION

The focus of this recipe is a statement made by Senator James Inhofe of Oklahoma during the March 21, 2007 hearing of the Senate Environment and Public Works Committee, at which the featured witness was former Vice-President, Al Gore. In his opening remarks, Senator Inhofe made a categorical statement essentially denying the reality of global warming. To support his position, Senator Inhofe cited a research article from *Science*. The exercise focuses on the question of whether Senator Inhofe used the information he cited correctly and ethically.

The purpose of this exercise is to drive home the point that statements of politicians, even when ostensibly based on the work of a respected scientist, must be verified. The value of teamwork is also promoted. Journalism majors have to be able to verify information independently of the original source.

COOKING TIME

Cooking time 60 minutes and serves no more than twenty sophomores.

ACRL INFORMATION DIETARY STANDARDS ADDRESSED

Standard One: 1.1, 1.4
Standard Two: 2.2, 2.3, 2.4
Standard Three: 3.1, 3.2, 3.4
Standard Five: 5.1

MAIN COOKING TECHNIQUE

- Pan sear a short 2 minute video clip.
- Stir in a brief PowerPoint presentation highlighting the relevant text of the statement.
- Simmer for 30 minutes in small groups working together at computers.

MAIN INGREDIENTS

- Computer/Internet access for students
- Teacher workstation with computer and speakers
- PowerPoint software
- Windows Media Player
- Video of Senate Environment and Public Works Committee of March 21, 2007, Senator James Inhofe's statement at EPW (http://www.youtube.com/watch?v=npimo1QK-4k)

PREPARATION

In any exercise of this kind, the instructor will want to make sure ahead of time that the information can be verified. This is the most time-consuming aspect of the preparation. Otherwise, there is little advanced preparation for this lesson. Prior to teaching, the video clip was downloaded as a file (as opposed to using YouTube.com live) and a short PowerPoint was created. Links to applicable online sources of information were established in advance. Most preparation time was spent in the classroom making sure the video clip would play properly.

Students will be prepared for this exercise by virtue of having had a course of instruction in library and information resources.

THE INSTRUCTION SESSION

1. **Introduction**
   a. Break students into groups of three.
   b. Short lecture focusing on the misuse of information, the distortion of factual information, and the need for a healthy sense of skepticism regarding information.

2. **Video clip**
   a. Show Inhofe video clip, providing students verbal cues for when they should pay specific attention.
   b. Display short PowerPoint. In the PowerPoint is a quote of Inhofe from the video. Inhofe is quoting research from Nature, Geophysical Letters, and Science.

3. **Team research**—30 minutes
   a. Students are told to use any means at their disposal to answer the question of whether Inhofe used the information he cited ethically.
   b. Students are given approximately thirty minutes for research and discussion within their groups.

4. **Report back**—15 minutes
   a. The students report on their findings and processes to the class.

ALLERGY WARNINGS

Students have a difficult time deciding where to start. One pattern of student behavior was to search for documents supporting Global Warming.

CHEFS' NOTE

The team approach was the right one. In most cases, the students did actually work as teams, bouncing around ideas for how to search, where to search, which databases to use, etc. In only one case did the students fail to work as a team; in that instance, each student worked on his or her own, with the result that they were not successful in reaching a conclusion. Those teams that did reach the correct conclusion did so in a variety of ways, showing skill in the use of the Internet and of scholarly databases. The students seemed genuinely confident in their ability to use information sources to accomplish a specific mission.

This example worked well, but it will certainly wear out over time. Therefore, it is a good idea to be on the lookout for fresh meat in the freezer section of your local Ethical Use of Information store.

Beaten and Whipped Bias

This recipe creates an opportunity for students to think critically about biased sources (while munching on homemade candy and playing with Play-Doh)

Monique Delatte, Librarian, Rio Hondo College Library, Whittier, CA, mdelatte@riohondo.edu

NUTRITION INFORMATION

This appetizer is a short exercise in teaching students to recognize that even seemingly unbiased resources and authors can present information in a one-sided manner. Biased Web sites are compared to typically unbiased library databases. Students are then challenged to think critically by viewing an entry in a library database that does present a bias.

COOKING TIME

Cooking time is 30 minutes. Serves a maximum of thirty students.

ACRL INFORMATION DIETARY STANDARDS ADDRESSED

Standard Three
Standard Four

MAIN COOKING TECHNIQUE

Teamwork, mini-demonstration

MAIN INGREDIENTS

- Computers for half of the class members
- Instructor's station
- Play-Doh
- Candy (for energy)!

PREPARATION

Place a portion of Play-Doh and a few pieces of candy in front of each student's seat. (This is especially appreciated by early morning classes.) This class is a good follow-up to database introduction classes.

Keeping students' hands busy while a teacher is talking can assist in learning. Mini-Play-Doh cans are cheaply available in Party Packs of ten. Adventurous librarian-chefs may want to homecook Play-Doh for the class beforehand.

Foodie-pedagogues may want to make your own candy.

THE INSTRUCTION SESSION

1. **Introduction**—15 minutes
   a. Discuss resources in which a prejudicial slant is prevalent, expected, or obvious, while your students munch rock candy, and surf the selected example Web sites.
   b. Discuss presumably bias-free resources while students use Play-Doh like a stress ball and visit the suggested databases. Share examples, such as the *American Decades* entry in *Biography Resource Center* about President Bill Clinton. This entry begins with the section

heading "Lost Opportunities," and is highly partisan in tone.

c. Challenge the students to find a more neutral entry in the *Biography Resource Center* within 5 minutes, working in pairs. The students will have to explain their answer.

2. **Group Challenge**—15 minutes

a. Challenge the group to find another example of bias in another seemingly bias-free database.

b. The first group to find an answer will win a prize, such as a copy card, gift certificates for thirty minutes of research personal training with a librarian, or candy. Or how about an apple for the student?

ALLERGY WARNINGS

Students may become frustrated after trying a few resources without success. To overcome this, provide personal assistance. Encourage students to use the entire allotted time.

CHEF'S NOTE

This piquant exercise will whet students' appetites for discrimination in selection of news information sources. Informally share more information, for example, ask if they've received e-mail, such as those analyzed at snopes.com. For example, "Did you get the mass forward about refilling your gas tank at the half-way point as a method of saving gas? Did it make sense to you?"

Students will appreciate the effort that you have dedicated to preparing this stimulating and pungent information literacy exercise. Enjoy the fruits of your labor.

Heat is key to confectionery consistency, so introduce the element of fire via team competition. Theoretically, we are teaching time-management, teamwork, and the most important lesson of all: 1 part library + 2 parts teamwork = consistently scrumptious results.

Bon appétit et laissez les bon temps rouler!

Apple-Flavored Hard Candy Recipe for a Hard-Working Researcher

Mix in glass bowl:
  ½ cup light corn syrup
  1 cup sugar

Cover with:
  Plastic wrap

Microwave for 3 minutes on high. Rapidly stir mixture, then recover with different plastic wrap and microwave for 3 more minutes.

After the mixture is no longer boiling, stir in:
  Green or red food coloring
  Apple extract

Pour syrup onto wax paper-covered cookie sheet or into non-stick molds. Let cool, store in plastic bags or airtight container, separated by wax paper.

Play-Clay Recipe for Pacifying Pupils

Mix over medium-to-high heat:
  1 cup flour
  ¼ cup salt
  2 tsp. cream of tartar

Mix in:
  1 tsp. oil
  1 cup warm water

Blend in:
  1 small bottle food coloring

Stir until smooth over medium heat. Remove from heat. Knead smooth. Let cool. Place in airtight container or plastic bags.

Succulent Rock Candy Recipe for Science-Centric Snacking

Heat in a medium saucepan:
  2 cups sugar
  1 cup water

Gradually stir in:
  2 more cups of sugar
  Food coloring

Once dissolved, pour into glass jar. Tie strings (cotton) to a pencil. Soak strings in sugar solution. Suspend the tips of the strings into the solution. Expose to sunlight for quick crystallization. Rock candy will grow for up to a week. Edible crystals will form within one hour.

Picking the Right Search Ingredients: Brainstorming and Evaluating Keywords in an Upper-level Psychology Course.

This recipe will help upper-level students understand that using different search terms can make a difference in their research.

Veronica Arellano, Psychology and Social Work Librarian, University of Houston, Texas, varellano@gmail.com

NUTRITION INFORMATION

In this recipe, students in a Child Development course must collectively create a literature review on Piaget's AB Error experiment. This recipe was developed to encourage students to really think about their research and all of the possible search terms and concepts they could use to effectively conduct a review of the scholarly literature.

COOKING TIME

Cooking time is 40 minutes. Serves up to fifty upperclassmen.

ACRL INFORMATION DIETARY STANDARDS ADDRESSED

Standard One: 1.1, 1.4
Standard Two: 2.1, 2.2, 2.4
Standard Three

MAIN COOKING TECHNIQUE

Class discussion and brainstorming, small group-work, hands-on practice

MAIN INGREDIENTS

- Computer access for all students
- Whiteboard or chalkboard

PREPARATION

It's helpful for the librarian to do some background reading on the literature review topic.

THE INSTRUCTION SESSION

1. Introduction
   a. Review the assignment with the students
   b. Briefly discuss the concept of the peer-reviewed journal article
   c. Introduce research resources available for psychology students
2. Brainstorming session
   a. Ask students to brainstorm possible search terms to use in the PsycINFO database
   b. Write all suggested search terms on the whiteboard
3. Group research
   a. Break the class up into groups
   b. Ask each group's leader to select one of the search terms on the board to use in their search
   c. Each group will try a search in PsycINFO using their selected search terms
4. Report back
   a. Have the group leaders report the number and relevancy of their results
   b. Write all results on the whiteboard
   c. Ask students to declare a winner
5. Individual research
   a. Students will then use the remaining class time to find a relevant article for their class

ALLERGY WARNINGS

- Students may initially have a difficult time with the brainstorming session. Therefore, it's very helpful to have one or two alternative search terms you can offer to get the ball rolling. literature review

CHEF'S NOTE

- Although the start to some brainstorming sessions can be a bit slow, once the students see a few synonym examples there is a general "Ah-ha!" moment and the alternative search terms start flowing like water.
- The searching competition has proven effective at showing students the difference a keyword can make. I've seen them erupt in surprise at receiving no results or hundreds of hits when using a particular keyword!

Chewing Over Cultures: Learning about New Languages and Cultures

Quickly immerse your students into country-related resources in the library using interactive teaching activities.

Suzanne Bernsten, Web Services Librarian, Lansing Community College Library, bernss@lcc.edu; Mary LaVigne, English as a Second Language Instructor, English Language and Culture Center, Lansing Community College, chezlavigne@aol.com

NUTRITION INFORMATION
This recipe will provide students with an introduction to library resources about language and culture and an opportunity to use the resources to learn about a country and the languages spoken there. This highly active recipe uses an icebreaker, bingo, and other activities

COOKING TIME
Cooking time is 60-90 minutes. Serves thirty students from an ESL, foreign language, nursing, or international business class; or study abroad students.

ACRL INFORMATION DIETARY STANDARDS ADDRESSED
Standard One: 1.1
Standard Two: 2.2, 2.3
Standard Three: 3.4

MAIN COOKING TECHNIQUE
Mini-demonstration, individual or small group work in computer lab

MAIN INGREDIENTS
- Computer access for all students
- Teaching station
- Handouts—Introduction to Library Resources and Research a Country
- Candy and healthy snacks for Bingo prizes

PREPARATION
Create handouts. Have candy or healthy snacks as prizes for the Bingo activity.

THE INSTRUCTION SESSION
1. **Quiz**—5 minutes
   - Ask students to guess what three languages (aside from English) are spoken by the most people in their city, county or state. Then present students with this data from the MLA Language Map— http://www.mla.org/census_main. This gets across the idea of language and cultural diversity in the local community even though the focus of the session is on countries other than the U.S.A.
2. **Icebreaker**—10 minutes
   - Students interview each other with prepared questions.
3. **Introduction to Library Resources**—20 minutes
   - Divide students into groups by row. Each row answers a question about a library or Internet resource. For example, students in Row One find a book from the library catalog about French. Then, one student in each row explains what they found.
4. **Culture and Language Bingo**—30 minutes
   - After students are introduced to library resources, they are told they will be leaving for the country of their choice in a few weeks and must answer questions about the country and the language(s) spoken there using library and Internet resources. The questions are arranged on a Bingo card. Each time students complete a row of questions, they receive a treat. Instructor circulates to answer questions.
5. **Wrap-up**—10 minutes
   - Debrief and answer any questions. Have students share one fact that surprised them from the Bingo activity.

ALLERGY WARNINGS

Students who have not encountered some of these resources become enthusiastic about specific databases and get caught up in exploring one without exploring others. Encourage students to explore a variety of resources to complete their task, and remind them they can return later to explore their favorites in-depth.

CHEFS' NOTE

Because this is an introductory session to some specific resources, it might be helpful to ask students at the beginning of the session what they hope to learn, and to ask during debriefing if their questions were answered. And if they were not answered, do they now know how to find that information? It is also a good idea to assess interest in a follow-up session.

Library Resources Handout

Each row answers a question about a library resource:

Row One—Library Catalog (books, CDs, DVDs)
Row Two—eAudiobooks (Pimsleur NetLibrary books for language study)
Row Three- Research Databases (Culturegrams, Ethnic Newswatch, World Geography)
Row Four—Web Sites (MLA Language Map, Ethnologue, Watching America)

Culture and Language Bingo Handout

Task for students:

You are leaving for _____ (country) in one month. Answer the questions below to prepare for your trip.

(Prepare questions about geography and climate, food and clothing, language, behavior and etiquette, and people.)

Icebreaker Handout

Students interview each other to find other students with specific language and cultural backgrounds, e.g. Find someone who ... speaks two languages

Emergency Preparedness Drill with Dessert

This recipe engages students in exploring evidence-based practice and emphasizes students' evaluation of health science resources as vital to quality patient care decisions.

Anne Marie Gruber, Assistant Director for Library Instruction and Public Services, Charles C. Myers Library, University of Dubuque, IA, amgruber@dbq.edu

NUTRITION INFORMATION

Newly-admitted nursing majors (juniors) have a full day of nursing program orientation and the library was asked to be part of it. This banquet focuses specifically on evaluating health resources available on the Web. The main course—Emergency Preparedness Drills—uses gaming methodology to encourage students to quickly answer research questions. Optional dessert is an introduction to health-related databases (e.g., CINAHL) to answer similar questions.

COOKING TIME

Cooking time is 45 minutes for the Emergency Preparedness Drills and another 30-45 minutes for the professional literature dessert. Serves a maximum of thirty nursing majors.

ACRL INFORMATION DIETARY STANDARDS ADDRESSED

Standard Two: 2.2, 2.3, 2.4
Standard Three: 3.1, 3.2
Standard Five: 5.1 (For follow-up dessert session)

MAIN COOKING TECHNIQUE

Peer collaboration, partner work in computer classroom, class discussion, game-based learning strategies include point-of-need instruction, practice before mastery, and individual adjustment

MAIN INGREDIENTS

- Computer with internet access for each pair of students
- Instructor station
- PowerPoint slides
- Blackboard/whiteboard

PREPARATION

Students should be familiar with basic internet research skills. Instructing librarian should gather three to four health science information examples and prepare PowerPoint slides with timed animation.

THE INSTRUCTION SESSION

1. **Introduction**—5 minutes
   - Librarian briefly introduces evidence-based practice concepts of using information to make quality patient-care decisions, follow appropriate and up-to-date procedures, and refer patients to quality consumer-health information.
2. **Emergency Preparedness Drills**—30 minutes (2 minutes to search and 8 minutes to discuss per drill)
   - Librarian divides class into pairs.
   - Librarian introduces the main course with the first Emergency Preparedness Drill, mentioning that there was an asthma study at Johns Hopkins University involving Ellen Roche, but not giving any additional detail.
   - Students work with their partner to use the Web to answer the open-ended question: What did research have to do with it? They must keep track of what sources they use and what evaluation criteria they considered.

- PowerPoint slides with timed animation count down each 30 seconds of search time (2 minutes total).
- Siren sound clip plays on transition to final slide of this drill. Students describe to the class what they discovered and what sources they used.
- Repeat steps for two to three additional health science examples. Urban legends, home remedies, internet hoaxes, or unbelievable-but-true health facts are ideal.
- Example topics: Freezing water in plastic water bottles releases toxic chemicals; antiperspirants cause breast cancer; sodium laureth sulfate, an ingredient in some hair care products, is carcinogenic.

3. **Group discussion about evaluation criteria**—10 minutes
   - Librarian facilitates student-lead discussion about evaluation criteria for health sciences information. Class works together to create a list of criteria that they determine is important to consider.

4. **Professional literature dessert**—30-45 minutes
   - Librarian wraps up drill session, by briefly reviewing applications for nursing professionals, before serving dessert. For a 75-minute session or an additional session with the same students, librarian transitions into discussion of professional nursing literature and how it differs from the free Web sources used in the drills. Librarian then introduces subject-specific databases (e.g., CINAHL) and allows pairs of students to practice searching using sample topics of their choice or from an assignment.

ALLERGY WARNINGS

- Students may protest about the short time limits.
- Students may be confused about what is expected at first, but giving them too much information defeats the student-led nature of the activity.
- The librarian needs to prepare topics before the session and be familiar with the free Web resources available, particularly for any topics that have unclear answers. Quality ingredients are a key part of the recipe!

CHEF'S NOTE

Both students and the librarian enjoyed this recipe! The peer collaboration made the session more effective for student learning, helping students brainstorm search strategies and discuss evaluation criteria with each other. The time limit on the drills gave the students a sense of urgency and motivated them toward effective and efficient Web searching with evaluation as a priority.

Nursing instructors liked the flavor too! The nursing instructors who observed were highly pleased with the engaging nature of the lesson, and following the session, one of them asked the librarian to provide them with some additional ideas for facilitating active learning in their classes. The session allowed the librarian to open broader discussions with faculty about incorporating higher-level research tools and strategies into the nursing curriculum. Further development may include incorporating an assignment into this orientation session and more formalized assessment of the information literacy skills addressed.

Thanks to Paul Waelchli (St. Norbert College) for the Drills idea, adapted from his library orientation session for football players, which uses fantasy football to discuss research and resource evaluation.

Armchair Analysis: Filleting Fictional Afflictions à la PsycINFO

In this recipe, psychology students role play a patient visiting a psychologist. After listening to disorder symptoms, the psychologist searches for articles in PsycINFO to help the patient.

Melissa Mallon, Library Instruction Coordinator, University of Pittsburgh at Johnstown, Johnstown, PA, mnmallon@pitt.edu

NUTRITION INFORMATION
The goal of this recipe is to familiarize students with the structure and scope of the PsycINFO database. This activity allows students the opportunity to get hands-on experience with the database by practicing searching techniques and finding relevant citations on a given topic.

COOKING TIME
Cooking time is 60 minutes. Serves thirty undergraduate psychology majors beginning a research project.

ACRL INFORMATION DIETARY STANDARDS ADDRESSED
Standard One: 1.1, 1.4
Standard Two: 2.2, 2.4
Standard Three: 3.7
Standard Four: 4.2

MAIN COOKING TECHNIQUE
Mini-demonstration, role play, small-group work (using computers), large-group discussion

MAIN INGREDIENTS
- Computer access for at least half of class
- Instructor workstation
- Blackboard/whiteboard
- Diagnosis Checklist handout

PREPARATION
You will need to make copies of the Diagnosis Checklist for each student and prepare a list of sample topics for students who can't come up with their own. It's also helpful to have a few searches prepared in advance, to use when demonstrating the database.

THE INSTRUCTION SESSION
1. **Introduction**—10 minutes
   a. Briefly demonstrate PsycINFO. Focus on its major functions, such as keyword searching and the Map Term to Subject Heading feature, setting limits, and combining searches with AND and OR. Have students work along.
2. **Role play**—30 minutes (students switch roles after 15 minutes)
   a. Split class up into groups of two (if odd number of students, a group of three is okay). Hand out a Diagnosis Checklist to each student.
   b. Assign one student as the Psychologist and one student as the Patient. Have the Patient describe to the Psychologist a condition that is afflicting them. Then have the Psychologist search PsycINFO for information on the disorder and possible treatments, filling out the Diagnosis Checklist as they go. Wander around the room to answer questions as they arise.
   c. Have the partners switch roles, and repeat the process.
3. **Discussion**—10 minutes
   a. Have entire class come together and discuss their findings. Write down successful keywords and search strategies on the board.

ALLERGY WARNINGS

- It may be difficult to get students into the creative mindset to come up with a fictional affliction, so be sure to have samples prepared.
- When the Patient is telling the Psychologist about their condition, make sure they use descriptive terms of their symptoms (other than just the name of a disorder) so the Psychologist will have plenty of keywords to try searching with.

CHEF'S NOTE

- It can take a little bit of time/coaxing to get students talking, but once they loosen up they seem to have fun in this low-stakes role playing situation. By switching roles halfway through, each student practices searching the database.
- Depending on the time allotted for the session, you many want to consider cutting down the number of items on the checklist. During the 60 minute session, it was a bit of a squeeze to get through the entire list and still have time for a good discussion. Another option would be to have the students switch roles halfway through the questions.
- This activity is great for engaging students, and I think it allows them to see PsycINFO in a more realistic context.

Diagnosis Checklist

Psychologist Name: _____

Patient Name: _____

1. Briefly describe the Patient's affliction:

2. With which keywords relating to the affliction did you start your search?

3. Which subject headings, if any, did you use?

4. Did you set any limits on your search(es)?

5. Which keywords and/or subject headings did you use to search for information on a treatment?

6. Did you combine any searches with AND or OR? If so, how?

7. List the citation for an article describing the disorder/affliction. Is it available full-text?

8. List the citation for an article related to treatment of the disorder/affliction (i.e. drugs, behavior therapy, etc.). Is it available full-text?

Brewing Literacy in the Chemistry Lab: Introducing SciFinder Scholar

SciFinder Scholar is a powerful but difficult to use database. This recipe uses demonstration and hands-on searching to introduce chemistry students to this tool.

Ignacio J. Ferrer-Vinent, Science Reference and Instruction Librarian and Assistant Professor, University of Colorado Denver, Auraria Library, ignacio.ferrer-vinent@ucdenver.edu

NUTRITION INFORMATION

The purpose of this recipe is to provide chemistry students with an easy, powerful way to search chemical literature for preparations of a substance and obtain empirical data that they can use to authenticate prepared compounds. The course assignment calls for the students to find a way to synthesize a specific compound and then check the results of the analysis of the compound with data from the literature about that substance, in order to insure that the desired compound was indeed prepared.

COOKING TIME

Cooking time is 60-120 minutes and serves approximately fifteen organic chemistry course students (typically sophomores and juniors).

ACRL INFORMATION DIETARY STANDARDS ADDRESSED

Standard One: 1.1
Standard Two: 2.1, 2.2, 2.4, 2.5
Standard Three: 3.2, 3.4, 3.6
Standard Four: 4.3

MAIN COOKING TECHNIQUE

Short demonstration, hands-on database searching, students working separately or in small groups

MAIN INGREDIENTS

- Computer with Internet access for each student
- Instructor station
- Subscription access to SFS

PREPARATION

- The organic chemistry professor will have already assigned a compound to be prepared in the chemistry laboratory. For the course assignment, the students will research this compound in SFS.
- Prepare a handout. I have created one I call "SFS Brief Users Guide."
- Permission from Chemical Abstracts Services for training-session access to SFS for all students during the scheduled session
- Pre-selected chemical compound name for demonstration
- Pre-selected chemical compound name for initial student exercise

THE INSTRUCTION SESSION

1. **Introduction**—10 minutes
   a. Do a short introduction about SFS and its capabilities.
   b. Do a demonstration of how to use one searching method within the database to obtain the desired information. [Brackets refer to the Web version of SFS.]
   c. Use *Locate/Locate Substances [Use Explore Substances/Substance Identifier]*
   d. For synthesis information—Use *A-B icon* [Use *Get Reactions*]
   e. For experimental data—Use the *Microscope* [Use *CAS Registry Number* or *Chemical Structure*—scroll down]

2. **Hands on**—15 minutes
   a. Give the students a simple exercise that provides practice of the method(s) you just demonstrated and builds their confidence.
   b. Select a compound that will result in a successful search, so students learn the mechanics of the search. Example: m-cresol or 4-bromophenol.

c. Ask the students to identify the oldest reference that reports on the compound's synthesis, the reported yield, and the IR spectra.

3. **Review the exercise for all to see**—2 minutes

4. **Compound search**
   a. Allow the students (separately or in groups) to search for the compound they will prepare in the laboratory. Circulate and be available to answer questions they might have. Ask the course professor to do the same, if possible.

5. **Conclusion**—10 minutes
   a. Regroup to see if the students got the information they desired. Remind them that SFS is available in the library for further research.

ALLERGY WARNINGS
- Students need to know that this is only one way of locating the needed information using SFS.
- Students need to realize that this is not an easy task. To find the best information they might need to spend more time.

CHEF'S NOTE
Students might think that they know how to search Google, however, SFS uses a very unique searching algorithm, quite different from most other databases. Once students get to see this powerful chemical database they are really excited about its capabilities.

Some chemistry professors who are not as accustomed to non-print sources are also amazed.

Cited Reference Searching: Who is Citing my Professor?

Students learn to search for cited references in Web of Science.

Sara Penhale, Science Librarian and Associate Professor of Biology, Earlham College, sarap@earlham.edu

NUTRITION INFORMATION

In this recipe, upper level students are introduced to the concept of cited reference searching as a technique for finding current scholarly literature. The students' interest is piqued by looking for citations to articles their professor has written. After conducting these training searches, students then repeat the procedure, using articles on their own topics that they identified ahead of time and brought to class.

COOKING TIME

Cooking time is 30 to 50 minutes.

ACRL INFORMATION DIETARY STANDARDS ADDRESSED

Standard One: 1.1, 1.2
Standard Two: 2.1, 2.2, 2.3, 2.4
Standard Three: 3.1, 3.2

MAIN COOKING TECHNIQUE

Short demonstration, hands-on

MAIN INGREDIENTS

- Student computer workstations with internet access.
- Instructor workstation
- Access to Thomson Reuters Web of Science

PREPARATION

Identify articles written by the course professor and select one that has been cited. If there are no papers meeting these criteria, choose papers written by someone else at the institution. Students should have chosen topics for a course assignment and identified one relevant primary research article. The article should be at least one year old in order to allow enough time for it to have been cited.

THE INSTRUCTION SESSION

1. **Demonstration**
   - Give each group the citation to an article written by the course professor.
   - Demonstrate a cited reference search in *Web of Science* and then ask the students to repeat the steps using the article they were given.

2. **Discussion**
   - As a group, discuss what they found and the cited reference search procedure.

3. **Hands-on**
   - Give the students the rest of the class period to research their own topics by conducting cited reference searches on the papers they brought to class. Encourage them to find as many relevant papers as possible in the allotted time.

ALLERGY WARNINGS

- Be sure to ask the professor ahead of time if you may use his or her articles in the cited reference search demonstration.
- Be prepared for some of the articles the students bring to class to have zero citations.

CHEF'S NOTE

- This instruction session is fun because students are interested in looking for citations to their professor's work. It provides an opportunity for the faculty member to talk about his or her scholarship or scholarly communication patterns in the discipline.

Close Encounters of the IL Kind

Students research the paranormal as an interest-grabber to create a persuasive presentation.

Ryan Sittler, Instructional Technology/Information Literacy Librarian and Assistant Professor, California University of Pennsylvania, California, PA, sittler@cup.edu

NUTRITION INFORMATION
This recipe is intended for students who are being asked to give a persuasive speech on a controversial topic of their choosing. Groups of students learn basic searching and topic organization by producing a short PowerPoint presentation.

COOKING TIME
Cooking time is a minimum of 60 minutes and serves a maximum of forty students.

ACRL INFORMATION DIETARY STANDARDS ADDRESSED
Standard One: 1.1.
Standard Two: 2.1, 2.2, 2.3.
Standard Three: 3.1, 3.3.
Standard Four: 4.1, 4.2, 4.3.

MAIN COOKING TECHNIQUE
Mini-demonstration, small-group work, peer assistance, presentations

MAIN INGREDIENTS
- Computer access (preferably laptops) for all students.
- PowerPoint software.
- An instructor's station with projector.
- A 2 gb flash drive.

PREPARATION
This session requires little advanced preparation, other than making yourself aware of the types of resources available to your students on the topics under discussion.

THE INSTRUCTION SESSION
1. **Introduction**—10 minutes
   a. Review assignment with students.
   b. Mention a few key resources for research purposes (catalog, databases, Web, etc).
2. **Group Work**—25 minutes
   - Group 1 will research alien abduction to prove that it is real.
   - Group 2 will research alien abduction to prove that it is fake.
   - Group 3 will research UFO sightings to prove that they are real.
   - Group 4 will research UFO sightings to prove that they are fake.
   a. Research must be supported by scholarly resources, appropriate Web sites are allowed.

   b. Each group will produce a PowerPoint presentation.
3. **Group presentations**
   a. collect presentations on Flash drive so that you may project them from the instructor's station.
   b. Groups present their findings.

ALLERGY WARNINGS
- Students may balk at their assigned viewpoint. Tell them that they may include a slide refuting their standpoint if they feel very strongly about the topic.
- Make sure that you have items in your collection that facilitate research on this topic. Scholarly books and articles DO exist.

CHEF'S NOTE
Most students groan at this topic. Most students also groan over the fact that they have to physically do something. However, past experience indicates that many students are willing to stay AFTER class if it means that they can out do the other groups. Ultimately, this becomes a very fun project. I have had it result in applause on more than one occasion. (It provides a good opportunity for student ingenuity.)

Does the Library Have Any Books About Women? Finding and Evaluating Sources About Female Movers and Shakers in the United States

This recipe provides tasty techniques for teaching basic level research on women's contributions to U.S. history and culture.

Sharon Ladenson, Gender Studies and Communications Librarian, Michigan State University, East Lansing, MI, ladenson@msu.edu

NUTRITION INFORMATION
In this recipe, first-year students enrolled in a composition course focusing broadly on *Women in America* are required to do a short research paper and presentation on a specific woman's influence and contribution to U.S. culture and society. Topics covered include: researching women's cultural, political, social and historical contributions; and the differences between primary and secondary sources.

COOKING TIME
Cooking time is a minimum of 60 minutes. Serves thirty first-year undergraduates.

ACRL INFORMATION DIETARY STANDARDS ADDRESSED
Standard One: 1.1, 1.2
Standard Two: 2.1, 2.2, 2.3, 2.4
Standard Three: 3.1, 3.2

MAIN COOKING TECHNIQUE
Individual and group work, group discussion, mini-demonstration

MAIN INGREDIENTS
- Computer access for all students
- Instructor's computer and projector
- Blackboard or whiteboard

PREPARATION
- Compile primary and secondary sources specific to a prominent woman of current popular interest
- Find a picture of the same woman
- Develop an online research guide

THE INSTRUCTION SESSION
1. **Introduction**
   - Show a picture of a prominent woman (e.g., Hillary Clinton) to the class.
   - Ask students to write down at least one question that they would like to ask about Hillary Clinton (or another prominent woman) and one information source in which they would expect to find the answer.
   - Elicit questions about Hillary Clinton and source ideas from students, and write them on the board.

- Discuss the difference between primary and secondary sources. Ask the students to identify which sources are primary, and which ones are secondary.

2. **Activity**—10 minutes.
   - Divide the class into five groups. Provide each group with a primary and a secondary source specific to Hillary Clinton.
   - Ask the students to compare and contrast the sources, and to identify which source is primary, and which one is secondary.
   - Groups should report their answers to the rest of the class.

3. **Demonstration**—10 minutes.
   - Distribute hard copies of the research guide.
   - Briefly show students a few key research tools presented in the guide for finding primary and secondary sources about women.

4. **Hands-on**
   - Ask students to write down a question that they would ask about another woman whom they would like to research.
   - Using the research guide, locate at least one source (either primary or secondary) in which they would expect to find the answer.

5. **Wrap-up**—10 minutes.
   - Ask students to share information on the sources that they found, and the research tools that they used to locate them.

ALLERGY WARNINGS

Finding sources on very obscure women naturally presents obstacles. Since this is an exercise in basic level research, work with the instructor to encourage students to choose a woman who strongly interests them, and who has been the subject of previous research, so that sources are available.

CHEF'S NOTE

- Having students write down their research questions and potential information sources allows them to think carefully about their answers before sharing them with the group. This helps to facilitate active and substantive participation.
- The exercise works quite well when using examples of women of current popular interest. During the 2008 U.S. presidential election season, I asked students to develop questions about both Sarah Palin and Hillary Clinton, which stimulated some lively discussion!
- Students appreciate the online research guide, for it points them directly to appropriate tools for finding relevant information. Providing ample time for the students to practice searching and exploring sources on their own is critical. Librarians should resist the temptation to demonstrate an extensive number of online and

print research tools, as this may overwhelm students. The key is to provide the students with sufficient information to facilitate starting their research, rather than exposing them to an exhaustive number of library and information resources.

Photos by Louis Villafranca.

Mashing Media Mentions of Scientific Studies: Tracing Newspaper Articles Back to Their Sources

In this recipe, students track mentions of scientific studies in the popular press back to their respective scientific journals.

Julie Gilbert, Academic Librarian and Assistant Professor, Gustavus Adolphus College, St. Peter, MN, jgilber2@gustavus.edu

NUTRITION INFORMATION

Students in an upper level women's studies class spend a large part of the semester analyzing media portrayals of women and gender. In this recipe, students track mentions of scientific studies in the popular press back to their respective scientific journals. This highlights the ways the press sometimes misconstrues scientific studies about gender.

In addition to addressing the subject content, the session provides students with the opportunity to use secondary sources to find primary sources, reinforces search strategies, and helps students evaluate how published information is used and interpreted by other agencies.

COOKING TIME

Cooking time is 60 minutes. Serves a maximum of twenty-five upper-level students.

ACRL INFORMATION DIETARY STANDARDS ADDRESSED

Standard One: 1.1
Standard Two: 2.1, 2.2, 2.3, 2.4
Standard Three: 3.1, 3.2, 3.4, 3.6

MAIN COOKING TECHNIQUE

Hands-on exploration in small groups

MAIN INGREDIENTS

- Computer access for all students
- Instructor's station
- Whiteboard/blackboard

PREPARATION

There are two options for preparation. The first option is more time consuming yet is more suitable for students with less library experience and/or for instruction sessions lasting less than one hour. The second option works well for longer sessions and senior students.

- Option One: Locate news articles about scientific studies on gender reported in the popular press. Check to see if your library has access to the journal publishing the original study.

- Option Two: Coordinate with the course instructor to have students gather examples of news articles ahead of time. Ask students to bring one example each to class; if the students work in groups, the group then has options if one example does not yield an accessible study. This approach also allows students to experience and reflect on the role of trial and error in the research process. Be prepared with a few backup articles just in case.

THE INSTRUCTION SESSION

1. **Introduction**—10 minutes
   - Introduce the activity, reminding students that the session will help them conduct similar research on their own, Also emphasize specific research tools.
   - Review the location of the primary research tools they will use and outline the steps they will take to conduct their research in these journal databases, including where to access full text articles. But do

not do a step-by-step tutorial of the process.

2. **Locate studies**—half of class time
   - Ask students to gather in groups of three or four. Give students at least half of class time to work in their groups to locate scientific studies in the databases. Circulate to answer questions and provide assistance.
   - Prompt students to examine the study and discuss the differences between the study itself and the news report.

3. **Report and discussion**
   - Ask groups to present their findings, focusing specifically on differences they noted between the study and the news report, as well as reflecting on the highs and lows of the research process.
   - This is a good opportunity to discuss with the entire class both the content they found and the research process itself.

ALLERGY WARNINGS

If students bring their own news articles to class, the library might not have the full text of the journal publishing the scientific study This is an obstacle that can be overcome if the students have other news articles to use. Even though students can become frustrated when they cannot immediately access an article, it provides an opportunity to highlight the

trial-and-error nature of research and prepares the students for the obstacles they might face when they conduct similar research on their own. This does slow down the process for some groups, however, and means some groups will get further ahead than others, as is often the risk in small group work.

CHEF'S NOTE

I had wanted to develop this assignment ever since helping biology students at the reference desk who were trying to locate scientific studies and examining how they were discussed in the press. It made sense to develop this with a women's studies class; students usually become very involved in the process, since they are motivated by finding out how the scientific

study differs from how it was reported. It's a bonus that they learn to trace sources and access journal articles along the way!

The next time I teach the session, I will collaborate more closely with the professor to determine the research sophistication of the students. If their professor feels they are less skilled at conducting research in the library, I will bring examples of articles I know will work instead of relying solely on the students to provide them, just in case the students provide no viable articles. I would also have them brainstorm with me places and ways to search, so that the entire class begins to formulate a research strategy instead of having it handed down from on high by me.

7. TECHNOLOGY

Blogging: Creating an Online Community

Blogs continue the academic discussion beyond the classroom.

Karla M. Schmit, Education and Behavioral Sciences Librarian, Penn State, and Assistant Director, Pennsylvania Center for the Book, kms454@psu.edu; Anne Behler, Information Literacy Librarian, Penn State, behler@psu.edu
Emily Rimland, Information Literacy Librarian, Penn State, elf113@psu.edu

NUTRITION INFORMATION

During the course session highlighted in this recipe, information was presented about an education database using *technology in education* as the topic to be researched. After the session, students used blogging as a way to reflect, and think critically on their previous school experiences with technology.

This session is one of a number of classes intended for undergraduate students taking a first year seminar course in library studies. The course examines the library, and provides the students with hands-on opportunities to experience the ways in which libraries acquire, organize, and make information available in all formats.

COOKING TIME

Cooking time for this recipe is one 40 minute class activity/presentation session. The discussion continues cooking outside of class as students write their blog, read classmate's blogs, and critically synthesize the information. Serves approximately twenty students.

ACRL INFORMATION DIETARY STANDARDS ADDRESSED

Standard One: 1.1, 1.2, 1.4
Standard Two: 2.1, 2.3, 2.5
Standard Three: 3.1, 3.2, 3.3, 3.4, 3.5, 3.6, 3.7
Standard Four: 4.1, 4.3,
Standard Five: 5.1, 5.2, 5.3

MAIN COOKING TECHNIQUE

Student reflection and learning through writing, reading and discussing blogs

MAIN INGREDIENTS

- Instructor's station
- Computers for each student in the class
- Individual blogging site (set up prior to first class)

PREPARATION

Develop a blog question for this session that reflects the topic of technology in education and also serves to spark student interest and reflection.

THE INSTRUCTION SESSION

1. **Technology in Education Class**
   a. Librarian demonstrates the features of an education database with the research topic: *Technology and Education*.
   b. Students follow the database demonstration at their own computer stations.
   c. Discussion of the kinds of articles that surface with the search terms, and ways to limit or increase the number of articles finding specificity within the broader topic.
   d. Discussion of technology in educational settings.

2. **Blog Assignment**
   a. Students receive the blog assignment related to the database demonstration, and discussion about technology as it is used in educational settings.
   b. Blog Assignment is as follows: Share a memorable school assignment from elementary, middle or high school that involved technology. What made it memorable? Was the assignment done

independently or in a group? Was learning the technology the important part of the assignment or was technology just an integral part of the productivity tools used in the learning process? How do you feel your early technology learning experiences influenced or affected your use of technology today? What emerging technology do you predict will most change how kids are schooled in the future?

3. **Assessment**
   a. The blog posts are one of the primary sources for the course grade.
   b. Each blog posting is worth 12 points.

4. **Blog Recap**
   Each week a group will be assigned to recap what was said on everyone's blogs during that week. Recap group will:
   - Briefly summarize the overall ideas and main point
   - Highlight a few favorite comments from the blogs or the most interesting points
   - Choose something thought provoking from the blog posts and pose it to the class for a brief discussion

ALLERGY WARNINGS

Students need to learn the etiquette of posting to an academic blog. For tips for students see http://blogger.psu.edu/help/basics/writingtips

CHEFS' NOTE

The blog assignment allows students to consider their past technology experiences and how it relates to their current technology use, and continued learning. It gives them an opportunity to reflect on the ways in which technology has influenced their understandings of information literacy in the past, the present, and how it may impact their learning in the future.

Grading Criteria for Blog Posting				
Each blog post you do for class is worth a maximum of 12 points. Your blog posts will be evaluated according to the following rubric:				
Components	3 points	2 points	1 point	0 points
On Time	Post is completed by 11:59 PM on Monday before class	Post is 1 day late	Post is 2 days late	Post is more than 2 days late or not completed.
Content	Post is on topic and relevant. Posts includes at least one link to a Web site/image/video/etc.	Post is on topic and relevant. Post does not include another link.	Post rambles off topic. Post does not include another link.	Post is incomplete or irrelevant.
Quality	Expresses two insights or reflections in your own words	Expresses one insight or reflection in your own words	Summarizes information but does not express reflections or insights	Post is incomplete or irrelevant
Mechanics	Effective use of spelling, grammar, or punctuation Uses a semi-formal tone.	Contains some errors in spelling, grammar, or punctuation. Uses a semi-formal tone.	Frequent errors in spelling, grammar, or punctuation. Uses a semi-formal tone.	Excessive use of jargon or slang. Tone is too informal for class.

Company Research: A "Clicker" Way to Do It

This recipe uses Clickers in a game format to test the abilities of student groups to present business information to their classmates. The librarian needs fast fingers, as the final quizzes need to be created as the students present.

Karen Anello, Business Research Librarian, Lippincott Library for the University of Pennsylvania's Wharton School, anellokj@wharton.upenn.edu; Mia Kirstien, Business Research Librarian, Lippincott Library for the University of Pennsylvania's Wharton School, kirstien@wharton.upenn.edu

NUTRITION INFORMATION

This recipe will give students the opportunity to explore library resources previously unknown to them, and to then present what they have learned to their peers.

Using our Business FAQ - http://faq.library.upenn.edu/recordList?library=Lippincott - we introduce students to the library's Web presence so that they will be able to locate appropriate databases for their research needs. We lead students through this knowledge databank of common reference questions in search of databases for specific types of materials. For example, we demonstrate a search for Analyst Reports.

COOKING TIME

Cooking time for this recipe is 60 minutes and serves thirty business undergraduate students.

ACRL INFORMATION DIETARY STANDARDS ADDRESSED

Standard One: 1.1, 1.2
Standard Two: 2.1, 2.2, 2.3
Standard Four: 4.1, 4.3

MAIN COOKING TECHNIQUE

Clickers, brief demonstration, group work, hands-on work, presentations

MAIN INGREDIENTS

- Computer access for all students
- Instructor's station
- PowerPoint Software
- Clickers, software, etc.

PREPARATION

- We prepare a short introduction to the library's Web page and the Business FAQ.
- The session quiz will be formulated on-the-fly as the students present their findings.
- Clicker technology must be tested prior to students' arrival and templates for the quiz should be prepared.

THE INSTRUCTION SESSION

1. **Introduction**
   - Discuss the assignment. (Define SWOT analysis.)
   - Show students how to navigate through the Web page, and demonstrate searching the Business FAQ.
   - Very briefly discuss the maintenance, history and purpose of the FAQ.

2. **Small group research**
   - Break class into three groups and explain that they will each be responsible for a certain aspect of company research. Each group will locate the appropriate databases, choose their favorite, and demonstrate how to find the required information to the other teams. As students do this, librarians will be available for assistance. Databases consulted will be chosen by each group from the FAQ.

- **Group 1** will be assigned Analyst (Investment Bank) Reports
- **Group 2** will be assigned Industry Reports
- **Group 3** will be assigned Company Profiles, Articles & News (potentially including some financials)
- Each group will produce a five-minute demonstration that will be given from the instructor's podium.

3. **Group presentations**
   - As each group is presenting, the librarians will be entering questions, based on the information the students give their classmates, into the clicker program in order to create a final quiz.

4. **Contest**
   - The contest will be given after all presentations and will be based on the results of the quiz.
   - The clickers will be given to the two teams observing each presentation, and the quiz will test the presenting group on how well they instructed the class.
   - The winning team will be the presenting group who produced the highest scoring quiz results. The winners will be rewarded.

5. **Conclusion**
   - The last few minutes of class will be devoted to questions, and to pointing out the librarian's contact information on the library's Web site.

ALLERGY WARNINGS
- The librarians should rove to keep students on task, and to be sure they are choosing appropriate data sources.
- Be sure the clicker technology is working and give ample time to set up and to test the technology.

CHEFS' NOTE
Undergraduates are often hesitant to present in front of their classmates. The contest provides an additional layer of competition that business students seem to respond well to. This is a light and fun activity with no wrong answers (clickers are not tied to students' identities) and with plenty of opportunity for students to explore on their own, rather than passively view our stale search examples. Plus, this gives them an opportunity to practice their public speaking skills in a low stress environment.

The Cite Is Right! A Game Show about Academic Integrity

This recipe presents an excellent use of Clicker technology. Students vote in reaction to cases and questions representing ethical academic decision making.

Laura Braunstein, English Language and Literature Librarian, Dartmouth College, lrb@dartmouth.edu

NUTRITION INFORMATION

This recipe begins a conversation with first-year students about institutional values and the norms and conventions of academic discourse. It provides an environment for discussing the ethics of scholarship, and helps students to understand the principles of proper citation.

The game show format allows students to discuss these serious issues in a fun, non-threatening environment. The Cite Is Right! can also be an opportunity to bring together several sections of the same course, with extended discussion in individual sections afterwards.

COOKING TIME

Cooking time is 60 minutes and serves a goodly number of first-year students.

ACRL INFORMATION DIETARY STANDARDS ADDRESSED

Standard Five: 5.1, 5.2, 5.3

MAIN COOKING TECHNIQUE

Clickers, question/answer, lively discussion!

MAIN INGREDIENTS

- Venue with computer and projector (two computers and dual projection are ideal but not mandatory)
- Clickers (personal response system devices), receiver, and software

PREPARATION

The instruction team (perhaps made up of a librarian, a faculty member, and an academic technologist) creates a series of case studies with follow-up questions. For example, some case studies might present a hypothetical situation and ask "Is this ethical?" while other questions might ask students whether a given citation is "Correct or Incorrect." In order to generate discussion among the group, case studies should have some ambiguity.

THE INSTRUCTION SESSION

1. **Group discussion format.**
   - Each student has a clicker.
   - After displaying and reading each question, the instruction team pauses to allow students to respond to the questions using the clickers.
   - When all the responses are in, the team displays the results on the screen.
   - Then, the team invites comments and reactions to the results.
   - After the discussion, the team can, if appropriate, discuss the rationale for the correct answer to the question.

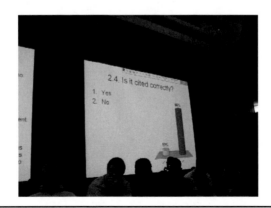

photos by Laura Barrett

2. Game show format

- For a large group combining several sections of the same course, the instruction team can call upon students to represent each section ("Come on down!") at the front of the classroom.
- These students will record their answers separately, before the whole group's results are displayed ("Survey says …?") and earn points for their section for correct answers.
- After several rounds of play, the section with the most points wins a small prize (e.g. gift certificates to a coffee shop).

ALLERGY WARNINGS

- Acquiring a sufficient number of Clickers, plus the receiver and software, may be a considerable investment for some libraries, but many computing and instructional-technology departments offer rentals or shared purchases. Many technologists are willing collaborators who are excited to participate in an innovative classroom application.
- On the practical level, a practice round at the beginning of the event may help assure students that their responses are being recorded.

CHEF'S NOTE

The audience response system (Clicker) technology has the potential to actively engage all students—each student must think through each scenario and submit a vote. The anonymity of the system accommodates multiple learning styles by allowing students to participate in the discussion without being singled out. Students who wish to offer comments and feedback to the group can be encouraged to do so throughout the event.

The instructional team should invite multiple perspectives and welcome debate among students. The Cite Is Right! offers an innovative model for other institutions looking for creative—and sometimes chaotic!—approaches to information literacy.

Special thanks to Karen Gocsik, Executive Director, Writing and Rhetoric Program, Dartmouth College; Sara Chaney, Instructor, Dartmouth College; and Barbara Knauff, Senior Instructional Technologist, Academic Computing, Dartmouth College. Some ideas for The Cite Is Right! were adapted from What's My Thesis? at Indiana University and Cornell University's Recognizing and Avoiding Plagiarism tutorial.

Sample Questions

1) *Case*: George is pulling an all-nighter to finish a History research paper and realizes that he forgot to write down where he found one of his most important quotations. After Googling and coming up with nothing, he decides to cite the source he thinks the quotation is from, throwing in a random page number.
     QUESTION: Is this ethical?

2) *Source material*: "When Aristotle (Poetics 23) wrote that description lends 'metaphorical life to lifeless objects,' he was demonstrating the close, often inseparable, connection between action-based description and figurative language. One often leads to another" (McClanahan 54).
The student writes: Aristotle says that an effective description gives life to inanimate objects through the use of metaphor (Poetics 23).
     QUESTION: Is the source cited correctly?

3) *Source material*: "Music points us to the central question here: how do we bind events in time? Spoken words are just like music: they exist in time, and we take them in by ear. Written texts may be laid out in simultaneous space, but good writers tend to heed, consciously or not, the fact that readers have an experience that is more temporal than spatial" (Elbow 625).
The student writes: Peter Elbow argues that students need help learning to give their readers "an experience that is more temporal than spatial" (625).
     QUESTION: Is the source cited correctly?

Do-It-Yourself Library Basics

Clickers can be used with more complex student questions. This recipe has students searching the catalog before responding.

Amelia Brunskill, Liaison Librarian for the Sciences, Dickinson College, Carlisle, PA, brunskia@dickinson.edu

NUTRITION INFORMATION

This recipe makes use of Clickers to give freshmen a first introduction to the library. Response slides include information about aspects of the library and various databases, providing opportunity for discussion of segments of information. This recipe is unusual in that questions require students to actually search the catalog, etc. before responding with their Clickers.

This was the first of three sessions for a first year seminar that focused on the ethics of hunting and fishing. The intention for this first session was to provide a broad introduction to identifying and locating materials owned by the library. The session was designed to make students as involved as possible so that they would become familiar and comfortable with this process, and a classroom response system played an important role here.

COOKING TIME

Cooking time is 30-50 minutes and serves ten to twenty–five freshmen

ACRL INFORMATION DIETARY STANDARDS ADDRESSED

Standard Two

MAIN COOKING TECHNIQUE

Clickers, hands-on experience

MAIN INGREDIENTS

- Instructor's station
- File of prepared slides
- Clickers (classroom response system)
- Slips of paper with specific journal and book titles
- Computers with access to the internet for all students
- Laminated maps of the library

PREPARATION

Create two lists of specific items that students should be able to physically locate in the library. Examples: relevant books that are not currently checked out and relevant journals owned by the library in print format. Print the lists and chop them into individual titles, so that there is a slip of paper listing a book title, and a slip of paper listing a journal title for each student.

Create response system compatible slides asking specific questions about library materials.

THE INSTRUCTION SESSION

1. **Interactive Clickers Quiz**
   a. Welcome the students to the session, and explain how the response system works.
   b. Open the first slide, which should serve as a gentle introduction to the system, such as a question about their previous experiences ("Have you ever used a college library before?") rather than a true quiz question.
   c. The next slide asks them whether they want to dive in and start answering questions or if they want some instruction first.
   d. The following slides ask them to answer some questions about the library's resources, typically requiring them to look up information about specific items, or use particular features of a given tool. Some questions require that they look at the map of the library in order to determine which floor an item would be located on, combining information about call number and named location in order to determine the resulting location. Example: On which level of the

library would the book *Disarmed* be located?

e. After each slide, review the correct answer, unless all of them responded correctly.

2. **Into the Stacks**
   a. After going through all of the slides, ask the students to look up their assigned book in the catalog.
   b. Have students locate their book and one volume of their assigned journal and bring them back to the classroom.

ALLERGY WARNINGS

Asking students to physically retrieve items often takes longer than expected. Allow at least double the amount of time that it would take for someone familiar with the library.

Freshmen are usually unfamiliar with the details of the Library of Congress Classification System, so explicit practice with the details of this system is important.

Expect that some students may not be able to locate their book without help.

CHEF'S NOTE

The students were active throughout the session, and the number of students correctly answering the questions provided useful insight into the amount of discussion necessary on various tools and concepts.

While the amount of initial prep work is considerable, once the session was underway there was comparatively little work necessary on the part of the instructor. As the session is so user-centered, instructors can gauge the level of difficulty that the class is experiencing with the material in a way that is unique to the particular class, rather than needing to rely on assumptions about what material would be obvious or confusing for the students.

TurningPoint was the classroom response system used, which worked well as it immediately compiles the responses from students, but other clicker technologies should work equally well. In the absence of a response system, one could simply ask students to locate the answers and then raise their hands in response to a list of choices or one could call on individual students.

Searching for a print journal will probably become less and less relevant as our subscriptions migrate online.

Clicker Crudité

This appetizer presents numerous opportunities to create mouth-watering and highly-interactive formative assessments that are immediately useful as you begin to teach.

Jenifer Sigafoes Phelan, Education Liaison/Remote Services Librarian, Seattle Pacific University Library, sigafoes@spu.edu

NUTRITION INFORMATION

This recipe can be added to any existing Information Literacy (IL) session to gather valuable information from attending students in order to help tailor the IL experience specifically to a level commensurate with their current knowledge level and frame of reference. In this activity, the librarian asks pointed questions in a quick, easy, and fun way before beginning the delivery of IL content. The information gathered will assist the librarian in tailoring the IL session specifically for the students present in the class.

COOKING TIME

Cooking time for this appetizer is 10 minutes. Recipe yield is limited to the number of PRS Clickers that are available.

ACRL INFORMATION DIETARY STANDARDS ADDRESSED

Standard Four

MAIN COOKING TECHNIQUE

Scaffolding—Determining your students level of IL knowledge and then building on it, quiz format, formative assessment

MAIN INGREDIENTS

- Instructor station with PRS software loaded
- Clicker hardware and software

PREPARATION

Create a list of multiple-choice or Yes/No (True/False) questions (generally a maximum of five will be sufficient) that will provide information about students' demographics or prior knowledge with the library and the library's resources. Be specific enough with the questions that they will prove useful when tailoring the impending IL session. Input your questions in to your PRS software and save the file in a spot where it can be accessed during the IL session.

Do a dry run prior to the students arriving, so there is time to solve any technology issue.

THE INSTRUCTION SESSION

1. While the students are arriving hand each a Clicker. It may be helpful to have a slide projected on the overhead that explains how to use the Clicker: how to turn it on, how to submit an answer, how to tell that your answer has been received, etc. This will save time during the IL session for covering content.
2. Once everyone is seated and you have welcomed the class and introduced yourself, explain that you have a few questions for them to answer to help you figure out how best to tailor the IL session to their specific needs.
3. Begin with a test question for them to practice with, for example "Is your clicker working? Yes/No." (Some wise guy will always say "no" even though their clicker is obviously working fine. ☺)
4. Now launch the prepared questions. After 100 percent of the group has answered each question, display the results for the group to see. This often prompts some interesting discussion but remember the time frame and keep chatting to a minimum.
5. Once you have received the information from the class make your mental notes about how to proceed from here and begin the content portion.
6. One thing you may discover is that a

sub-section of your class is very new to library resources while the majority is knowledgeable. If you have the luxury of a break during your IL session, you may want to prompt the students new to the library to join you then for a mini-session to answer their specific questions instead of discussing basic information in front of the whole group. Or recommend they make an appointment with you at a later date/time.

ALLERGY WARNINGS
Wait until the entire student audience has responded before displaying the chart showing how the group as a whole responded. Students will start migrating their answers to match the group consensus if the chart is displayed too early.

A way to alleviate technology problems is to have the PRS presentation questions loaded and run on a secondary computer, i.e. laptop if available, while the librarian's main presentation is made on the primary computer. In this instance a projector input switching device may be necessary.

CHEF'S NOTE
There are many benefits of teaching with a PRS System.

For the students, the "Wow-Factor" of using handheld technology is cool and the ability for them to respond anonymously allows a safe environment in which they may be more willing to admit they haven't got a clue about something while not looking stupid in front of their peers.

For the librarian it allows the quick and easy gathering of a lot of valuable information in a relatively short period of time. The PRS software can gather the information into a spreadsheet that can be saved for later viewing. These files can be used to assess all sorts of things. One example: every time the students from EDU 6982 Educational Inquiry arrive they know all about the ERIC database but do not even know the library subscribes to Mental Measurements Yearbook online or even what it is. This allows the librarian to examine points in the curriculum where the Master of Arts in Teaching program intersects with library instruction and potentially adjust what IL skills these students are learning earlier on in their course work. It will also provide a librarian with hard evidence when presenting to a School or Department about the need for further library instruction opportunities for their students.

The PRS Clickers can also be used for pre- and post-tests during IL sessions. Perhaps ask content questions up front and follow the session with the same content questions again to see what the students have learned. The assessment options with a PRS System are limitless.

The PRS can be used to hold students' attention during a session by asking check-for-understanding questions as the session unfolds. This works as a good alert system for the librarian if a topic warrants some more time before moving on. Hey, if you already have the PRS system up and running and each student has a clicker for an appetizer activity, you might as well consider the other things you can do during the session.

Caramelizing Classroom Community with Clickers

Tired of the same, old three-squares a day routine? Want to jazz up your Information Literacy Instruction? Try our easy Clicker recipe and watch the family come alive!

Krista Prock, Information Literacy Librarian, Kutztown University of Pennsylvania, prock@kutztown.edu
William Jefferson, Learning Technologies Center Coordinator, Kutztown University of Pennsylvania, wjeffers@kutztown.edu

NUTRITION INFORMATION

Seriously, folks, students expect IL sessions to be boring. Clickers add a fun, interactive game-show type feel to your sessions. Clicker questions integrate easily into your PowerPoint lectures and using the Clickers in class is a snap. Try it you'll like it. More importantly your students will too.

COOKING TIME

Cooking time varies depending upon your presentation. Serves a large group especially well.

ACRL INFORMATION DIETARY STANDARDS ADDRESSED

Clickers are like a multivitamin; they can be used to enhance (or assess) all five Standards.

MAIN COOKING TECHNIQUE

Clickers, (lecture/demonstration assessed every 5-7 minutes with a Clicker question or activity), formative assessment

MAIN INGREDIENTS

- Students
- Clickers
- Subject - The one ingredient that can be substituted in this recipe is the subject. The Clicker technique can be applied to any subject.

PREPARATION

- Develop an Information Literacy PowerPoint presentation.
- Add Clicker questions (season to suit your taste).
- Stir.
- Have a co-worker sample your recipe before serving your main course to students.

THE INSTRUCTION SESSION

1. Start by distributing Clickers to all students and showing everyone how they work. Have a simple question ready that everyone can answer and practice using their Clicker.
2. Begin the PowerPoint presentation.
3. Talk about the library, how students can access services, and where students can find help.
4. Intersperse the lecture with questions that reinforce the ideas being shared with the students.

ALLERGY WARNINGS

Technology phobic librarians rejoice. There are no known allergic reactions to be concerned about. Try it; you'll be amazed at how easy it is to use Clickers in the classroom.

CHEFS' NOTE

Clickers are useful for maintaining student interest and assessing student learning. Good questions are difficult to write, but once they are written Clickers can be used to assess student learning in a one-time information literacy class. The librarian can get a sense of student understanding even if no one chooses to speak up.

Linking Citations to the Virtual World: Folding *Facebook* into Scholarship

This recipe for upperclassmen uses Facebook as a starting point to explain citation linking.

Deborah Hicks, Public Services Librarian, University of Alberta, Edmonton AB, deborah.hicks@ualberta.ca
Virginia Pow, Public Services Librarian, University of Alberta, Edmonton AB, virginia.pow@ualberta.ca

NUTRITION INFORMATION
In a hands-on session students research *Facebook* as software that connects people. Students then repeat the same exercises using Web of Science which connects scholars.

COOKING TIME
Cooking time is 50 minutes.

ACRL INFORMATION DIETARY STANDARDS ADDRESSED
Standard One: 1.2
Standard Two: 2.1, 2.2, 2.3, 2.4

MAIN COOKING TECHNIQUE
Mini-lecture, small-group work, peer assistance, discussion

MAIN INGREDIENTS
- Computer access for students
- Teaching station
- Facebook account and Web of Science database

PREPARATION
You will need to work through some of the citation chains/citation links ahead of time, as well as create a *Facebook* account.

THE INSTRUCTION SESSION
1. **Introduction**—5 minutes
   a. Mini-lecture on citation linking.
2. **Facebook Activity**—10 minutes
   a. Assign each group a different task.
      - Connect from home profile to a profile in another predetermined country
      - Connect a profile to the largest corporation they can find using the friends list
      - Browse the college network's members using limits such as interest
      - Connect profiles using group memberships
      - Connect profiles using applications, such as Catbook
      - Connect profiles through photos
      - Connect profiles through education information, etc.
3. **Facebook Discussion**—10 minutes
   a. Have students report back.
4. **Web of Science Activity**—10 minutes
   a. Assign each group a task.
      - Find a major paper. Note the number of times it has been cited. What is the oldest citation? What discipline cites it the most?
      - Move from a paper in one discipline to a paper in another discipline using only citations
      - Move from author to author
      - Move from journal to journal
5. **Web of Science Discussion**—10 minutes
   - Have students report back.
6. **Conclusion**
   - End with a short discussion about how citation chaining will help them in their research. Draw on allusions to the Facebook and Web of Science searches.

ALLERGY WARNINGS
Students may not see the relevance to citation linking/citation chaining at the beginning. Tell them this can be a very useful and time saving tool for their research.

CHEF'S NOTE
Most students are unaware that citation linking/citation chaining is a valid research tool; this session is to help create awareness for the students.

Assessment à la mode: Online Survey

This dessert is an assessment that does not take precious time away from instruction. Instead, student learning is measured with online survey software after the class is over.

Jenifer Sigafoes Phelan, Education Liaison/Remote Services Librarian, Seattle Pacific University Library, sigafoes@spu.edu

NUTRITION INFORMATION

This dessert provides an opportunity for the librarian to gather evidence that the class learned the skills taught and/or evaluative data about how the students perceived the session via an online survey.

COOKING TIME

Cooking time is 10 minutes. Use a maximum of ten questions.

ACRL INFORMATION DIETARY STANDARDS ADDRESSED

An online survey can be used by any savvy librarian to assess most cognitive learning outcomes.

MAIN COOKING TECHNIQUE

Student feedback for evaluation/assessment purposes, summative assessment

MAIN INGREDIENTS

- A computer with Internet access
- Online survey tool (examples: SurveyMonkey or Zoomerang)
- A list of your student participants' e-mail addresses

PREPARATION

Permission - First and foremost, ask the professor's permission to send their students an online survey. This is also a good time to request a class roster that includes e-mail addresses. Professors usually say yes but appreciate being asked.

Online Survey Preparation - Before teaching the session to be evaluated, it will be necessary to compile a list of questions you would like the students to answer after the session occurs. Decide whether the questions should be content questions, evaluation questions, or a mixture of both. Also, decide if you want to ask multiple-choice questions, open-ended questions, or a combination. Writing the questions while preparing to teach the session will help ensure they are directly tied to the content covered and the type of evaluation feedback desired.

THE INSTRUCTION SESSION

1. **When to send the assessment**
   - Decide strategically when to deploy the survey. To get a high number of responses, it may be best to send it moments before walking to the session so you can tell the students it will be waiting in their boxes the next time they check their e-mail.
   - It may also suit your objectives to tell the students you want them to practice their new IL skills and complete the class assignment prior to deploying the survey. To these groups of students, explain that in one week when their assignment is due on Wednesday there will be a follow-up online survey e-mailed out on Thursday.

2. Types of questions

- Sending the survey after the assignment is due allows for questions, such as: "Which databases ended up being the most useful for your project topic?" "Was the information you learned in the library session helpful when you conducted your research?" or "What did you have trouble remembering how to do later when you were sitting at your own computer conducting research?"
- Content questions can also be informative in the assessment process as a check for understanding: "What does ILL stand for and what can you use it for?" "What databases did the librarian recommend for your project?" or "How do you limit your search in the ERIC database specifically to locate primary research articles?"

3. Online instruction

- If deploying with students in an online environment use the course software "Announcements" section to post an announcement that says, "You will be receiving an online survey in your university e-mail account today. Please take a moment to fill it out. Your responses help make the library's instruction program stronger."

4. Response rate

- For all online surveys, if there is low response, it may be necessary to send out one reminder e-mail to those who have not yet completed the survey a few days after the initial e-mail is sent. No more than one reminder should be sent.
- While it is important for students to know there is a dessert available, remember some individuals are on diets and may choose to skip dessert. That is ok.

ALLERGY WARNINGS

The response rate may be low. Typically online surveys have a response rate under 30 percent or even lower. Learn to cherish the responses that do come in. They are valuable. Remember many universities have moved to an online format for all of their course evaluations, so why not librarians too?

CHEF'S NOTE

Online surveys are an excellent way to reach out to extended communities of students such as the ones who receive library instruction through online course software. While in-session paper forms have a high response rate in face-to-face settings, they take time away from instruction and require compilation into electronic format after the session is over. Switching to an online survey will maximize IL session time while minimizing librarian time collating student responses. Online survey software can usually produce charts and graphs for multiple-choice questions that look good when included in librarians' files for review, promotion, or tenure.

Toasting Tags and Cubing Keywords with Flickr Photos: Flickr Keywording/Tagging Exercise

Tagging Flickr photos is used as a scaffold to understand the concept of creating keywords.

Nancy Noe, Instruction Coordinator, Auburn University, noenanc@auburn.edu

NUTRITION INFORMATION
This appetizer relates tagging photos in the popular Flickr Web site to brainstorming keywords for a search topic. Students participate in tagging images, developing synonyms, and repeating strategies with their own topics.

COOKING TIME
Cooking time for this appetizer is approximately 30 minutes and can be themed to a specific class or assignment. Serves fifteen to thirty underclassmen.

ACRL INFORMATION DIETARY STANDARDS ADDRESSED
Standard One: 1.1
Standard Two: 2.2

MAIN COOKING TECHNIQUE
Brainstorming

MAIN INGREDIENTS
Internet access
Instructor's workstation
Student workstations

PREPARATION
Select a photo from Flickr that has some relevance to the class theme or assignment. Save the picture (without tags) on a flash drive or desktop for presentation.

THE INSTRUCTION SESSION
1. Librarian brings up the pre-selected photo related to class theme or assignment on screen for class to see.
2. Librarian introduces Flickr and class is asked to construct a tag (keyword) list—words, synonyms, and phrases that best describe the photo - which the librarian writes on the board.
3. Librarian gives students 3-5 minutes to see who can find the photo on Flickr first. (That student wins a fabulous library prize.)
4. Class compares their tag list with that of the list on Flickr (What did we miss? What words were alike? Did we think of this synonym?)
5. Librarian explains that tagging the photo is very similar to what students should do to their topic before they begin to search.
6. Class is given 10 minutes to tag their topics with librarian and instructor checking on individual student progress.

7. Librarian then goes to a general database, solicits examples of topics from students, and demonstrates a general database search.

ALLERGY WARNINGS
It often takes time to locate a Flickr photo that is interesting, relevant or provocative with enough tags so that students won't immediately think of.

As to not violate fair use, we have decided not to use the same image for more than one class.

CHEF'S NOTE
Students enjoy the competitive nature of the activity. Pairs well with focusing and narrowing search strategies.

QuickWiki: Constructing a Collaborative Cassoulet

A collaborative wiki can help students think critically about: library research, evaluating sources, revising their writing, and the nature of scholarship in academic communities.

Laura Braunstein, English Language and Literature Librarian, Dartmouth College, lrb@dartmouth.edu

NUTRITION INFORMATION
This diagnostic recipe helps the students, the librarian, and the professor understand what background the students bring to the session in order to use that knowledge to help the students evaluate resources effectively.

COOKING TIME
Cooking time occurs primarily before your follow-up session. Follow-up discussion session is 60 minutes. Recipe serves thirty freshmen.

ACRL INFORMATION DIETARY STANDARDS ADDRESSED
Standard One: 1.1, 1.2
Standard Two: 2.3, 2.5
Standard Three: 3.1, 3.2, 3.6
Standard Four: 4.3
Standard Five: 5.3

MAIN COOKING TECHNIQUE
Lively discussion during the instruction session, collaborative writing before the class begins, wiki

MAIN INGREDIENTS
- Instructor workstation
- Student computers
- Wiki software (embedded in courseware or Web-based)

PREPARATION
It's always important to collaborate with a faculty member who is enthusiastic and willing to experiment with an open-ended, diagnostic assignment!

THE INSTRUCTION SESSION
1. **Before the session**
   - Students read a common text. Before the class meets with the librarian, the students use the wiki to make a list of terms that they need to know in order to understand the text.
   - The class writes collaboratively, using the wiki to define these terms. As they work, the students are encouraged to revise their peers' entries in order to create a collaborative resource. They may use any credible source, but they must cite the sources.
2. The session
   - The librarian reviews the wiki before class and selects items from the Sources page.
   - As the librarian posts the items for review, she asks the class a number of discussion questions:
     a. Why is this source credible?
     b. To whom is it credible? Who is the audience? Who wrote or created it?
     c. What criteria did you use to evaluate it?
     d. Is this an academic source? Why and when do we use academic sources?
     e. How did you find it?
     f. Is this the correct way to cite this source?

ALLERGY WARNINGS
In order to encourage participation, the professor or the librarian can show how the wiki software tracks participants (as well as the time, date, and extent of their contributions).

CHEF'S NOTE
The assignment can reveal how students construct knowledge, how they find and evaluate sources, and how they make sense of material they've never seen before—all crucial steps in the learning process and the development of information literacy.

Special thanks to Karen Gocsik, Executive Director, Writing and Rhetoric Program, Dartmouth College.

Whipping up Webcasts

Enter the greener pastures of grassroots video and cast your own webcast.

Lisa Gieskes, School Media and Internet Public Librarian, lisagieskes@yahoo.com

NUTRITION INFORMATION

According to the 2008 Horizon Report, grassroots video and collaboration Webs are two of six emerging technologies most likely to be widely used in the field of education. Educators are creating their own specially branded media, allowing for community-generated content along with institutional video offerings. This demonstration is intended to show educators and their students how to create their own Webcasts for use in the classroom.

The New Media Consortium. "The Horizon Report." 2008. http://www.nmc.org/pdf/2008-Horizon-Report.pdf.

COOKING TIME

Cooking time is approximately 120 minutes and serves a small class.

ACRL INFORMATION DIETARY STANDARDS ADDRESSED

Standard Four

MAIN COOKING TECHNIQUE

Mini-demonstration, small-group work in computer lab, camera, microphone, recording and editing software

MAIN INGREDIENTS

- Computer access (preferably laptops) with high speed Internet for all participants
- Camera, etc.
- Script

PREPARATION

Participants should have chosen Webcast topics with necessary resources before the session.

THE INSTRUCTION SESSION

1. Ask group participants to describe the specifics of their topic to the whole class
2. Get each group to write and share their script
3. Provide a mini-demonstration
4. Allow groups to record their own Webcast and circulate to answer questions
5. Reserve the last ten minutes for debriefing as a group

ALLERGY WARNINGS

Participants may first be nervous about presenting before a group, but once separated into teams, become enthusiastic about their collaborative work.

CHEF'S NOTE

There is usually one extrovert in each group. Seek this person out and make them the Webcast model.

MacBookPro Webcasting

MacBookPro computers with built-in Webcams, microphones, and iMovie software are ideal for this project. It is easy to create a video in iMovie. Click on File and select New Project in order to create a new project in your Project Library. To start filming select the Projector icon. This will bring up your camera, with audio. Begin to record and capture your movie. You can then edit it afterwards (adding your title or sound effects from the vast built-in library). You can save this project by clicking Done. Share to YouTube for video on demand.

Live Webcasting

It is possible to produce a live Webcast using ustreamtvonline at http://www.ustream.tv. This free hosting service will allow you to broadcast live video on the Web.

About the ~~Editors~~ Chefs

Chef Ryan L. Sittler is the Instructional Technology/Information Literacy Librarian, and an Assistant Professor, at California University of Pennsylvania. He received his MSLS from Clarion University of Pennsylvania in 2005 (he is currently an adjunct Instructor in their Department of Library Science) and received his Master of Science in Instructional Technology from Bloomsburg University of Pennsylvania in 2008. He is currently working on a Ph.D. in Communications Media and Instructional Technology at Indiana University of Pennsylvania.

Ryan's previous publication with Doug Cook, *Practical Pedagogy for Library Instructors: 17 Innovative Strategies to Improve Student Learning*, has garnered positive attention and he hopes that this book is equally well received.

When he isn't writing, working, or studying, Ryan can be found engaging in one of many hobbies—lately, this includes teaching himself to play piano or playing irresponsible amounts of Rock Band 2. (Gamertag: rlsittler.) He also welcomes opportunities to engage in consulting work in instructional design—especially as it relates to information literacy. You may contact him by e-mail at sittler@calu.edu or rlsittler@aol.com.

Chef Ryan L. Sittler

Chef Douglas Cook, D.Ed., is a Reference Librarian and Professor at Shippensburg University of Pennsylvania. He received his MLS from the University of Maryland and his doctorate from the Pennsylvania State University. He is most interested in library cookery as seen through the eyes of students. How can we motivate and engage students in sharpening their information research appetites?

This *Cookbook* is his third edited book of pragmatic advice for library instructors. With Tasha Cooper, he edited the book, *Teaching Information Literacy Skills to Social Science Students and Practioners* (Chicago: ACRL. 2006). And with Ryan L. Sittler he edited the book *Practical Pedagogy for Library Instructors: 17 Innovative Strategies to Improve Student Learning* (Chicago: ACRL. 2008).

When Doug is not out taking his Garmin GPS unit and his Sony digital camera for a walk in Michaux Forest he may be contacted by e-mail at dlcook@ship.edu dr_library_guy@yahoo.com.

Chef Douglas Cook